**First Alabama Bank
of Montgomery, N.A.**
Post Office Box 511
Montgomery, Alabama 36101
Telephone 205 832-8140

Jack Eley
Senior Vice President

September 29, 1980

TO WHOM IT MAY CONCERN:

Re: Mary S. Relfe
     Montgomery, Alabama

..."A most valued client of First Alabama Bank.
I would not hesitate to enter into any venture
with her that she considers to be sound.

...I have watched her grow in the various business ventures that she is in, all of which, I
might add, have been most successful.

As to her character and personal habits, I
can attest to them being impeccable.

I feel that I have gained much more from
knowing Mrs. Relfe these past sixteen years
than she has ever gained from the advice
that I have given to her."

Excerpt taken from letter of Mr. Jack Eley, Senior Vice President,
First Alabama Bank, Montgomery, Alabama.

THE NEW

MONEY SYSTEM 666

Mary Stewart Relfe, Ph.D.

The Publisher endeavors to print only information from sources believed reliable, but absolute accuracy cannot be guaranteed.

Information in this book is not an indictment against any product, person, or institution, financial or otherwise; but simply evidence of Bible Prophecy being fulfilled in this final World System.

First printing — February, 1982
Second printing — February, 1982

Copyright ® 1982 by Ministries, Inc.
P.O. Box 4038
Montgomery, Alabama 36104
U.S.A.

ISBN 0-9607986-1-7

Printed in the United States of America

DEDICATION

To my only child, Anthony, my son, my
son, whose life was taken suddenly in
a tragic industrial accident.

August 8, 1952 — May 13, 1980

And, to all my sons and daughters whom
the Lord has given me in the faith, from
bankers to bar maids, who have written
expressing their acceptance of Jesus
Christ as a result of reading my first
book, *WHEN YOUR MONEY FAILS*.

APPRECIATION

- DR. C.M. WARD, who assisted me in writing the Newsletter, that more time could be devoted to the writing of this book.

- JOHN H. SHEPHERD, who obeyed the Lord, and mailed to me data pertinent to this book.

- THE REV. HAROLD KELLY, who supplied me with some much needed information.

- ALL OF YOU who have mailed clippings, books, pictures, etc., relating to fulfillments of Bible Prophecy. Keep it up.

- BERNARD STEWART, my brother, who directed the publishing and distribution of the first book, and Newsletters, that I could spend my time in study.

- SALLY O'BRIEN, the friend closer than a brother, without whose prayers, encouragement, patience, and daily assistance, this work would have never been completed.

- Artwork by Charlotte Trosper

- Photographs by Linda White, Sally O'Brien, and Harold Kelly

BULLETIN OF
THE ATOMIC SCIENTIST

January 1980
Seven minutes
to midnight ...

January 1982
Four minutes
to midnight

"We feel impelled to record and to emphasize the accelerating drift toward disaster in almost all realms of social activity. Accordingly, we have decided to move the hands of the Bulletin's Clock — symbol of the world's approach to nuclear doomsday — forward from seven to four minutes before midnight."

Each minute represents a year. Midnight represents nuclear disaster.

Why does this elite but secular group of scientists know more about the end of the age than the Church?

> *"The children of this world are wiser ... than the children of light."*
>
> Luke 16:8

"THE LORD GAVE ME THIS ANSWER: 'WRITE DOWN CLEARLY ON TABLETS WHAT I REVEAL TO YOU, SO THAT IT CAN BE READ AT A GLANCE."

Habakkuk 2:2
Good News Bible

"AND MONEY CAME TO PASS,
IT DIDN'T COME TO STAY."

Mary Stewart Relfe

PROPHETIC PORTENT OF THINGS TO COME!
This advertisement appeared in the Palo Alto Times, March 3, 1981.

"And he causeth all, both small and great, rich and poor, free and bond, to receive a MARK in their right hand, or in their foreheads: And that no man might BUY OR SELL, save he that had the MARK, or the name of the beast, or the NUMBER of his name. Here is wisdom. Let him that hath understanding count the NUMBER of the beast: for it is the NUMBER of a man; and his NUMBER is Six hundred three score and six." Revelation 13:16-18

PREFACE

THE THRUST OF THE FIRST BOOK I WROTE, *WHEN YOUR MONEY FAILS . . . THE 666 SYSTEM IS HERE*, was to find a common bond between Government debts, hyperinflation, the collapse of economies, the worthlessness of currencies, electronic money, and the emergence of a World Wide Card with which to conduct commerce. The thread woven throughout this chain of events proved to be the usage of the Number "666." Dozens of usages were both discussed and pictured by many segments of industry, from banking to communications, from manufacturing to retail.

As a successful business person of many years, I had become a keen observer of economic trends. As a student of Bible Prophecy, I was able to identify a positive drift toward the last Economic Regime about which the Prophet John had said would be UNIVERSAL, CASHLESS, CONDUCTED WITH "MARKS," and, through this unique System of "buying and selling" control would be gained over the Political and Religious Disciplines of the World. However, in the first book, I could only define broad outlines of a loosely knit World Federation promoting the consensus of "Internationalism" through the open and broad usages of the Number "666." For example, I would discover it on a flashlight manufactured in West Germany; on shoes made in Taiwan, on a key imprinted in the United States, and on bank Cards in Austrailia. And while these do not exhaust my research, I use this grouping to indicate that there seemed to be no common denominator or corporate identity to be uncovered in any of these organizations. Furthermore, I was unable to pinpoint any one giant conglomerate, national or multi-national, most reponsible for the "666 phenomenon" of the decade of the 1970's.

But God made Revelation progressive! While we see through a glass darkly, we do see! And we see clearer in this decade of the 80's than we saw in the 70's. We have moved into closer proximity with these events, and those specks of dust we were discerning in the 70's have turned out to be the pillars upon which this entire End-time System is structured.

THE THRUST OF THIS BOOK, *THE NEW MONEY SYSTEM, and 666*, is to discuss:

- How Bar Codes "MARKS" for PRODUCTS, PLACES and PEOPLE are becoming the Universal System of IDENTIFICATION for purposes of "buying and selling."

- As *Items* are now identified by Bar Codes, *Personal Identification* is being converted to Bar Codes.

- The "Coded" use of "666" in the Universal Product Code "Bar Code," etc.

- The identity of THE CONSORTIUM PROMOTING THE GLOBAL USE OF "666," and expand upon the users of this Number to include HEADS OF NATIONS, DEPARTMENTS OF GOVERNMENTS, RELIGIOUS ORDERS, and WORLD ORGANIZATIONS.

- ELECTRONIC FUNDS TRANSFER (THE CASHLESS) SYSTEM IS DESIGNED TO REMOVE ALL MONEY FROM INDIVIDUALS; BUT, BY SO DOING, WILL ELIMINATE ALL PERSONAL FREEDOM AND PRIVACY.

- As every person, place and thing come under the Identity and Control of this "Bar Code Marking System," the Chief Architects of this Consortium will realize the fruition of their ulterior motive; THE NEW MONEY SYSTEM; "Marks" for people; "Money" for them.

The first book was about the Number. This book is about the Mark, and how the Mark incorporates the Number.

The Prophet John identified this Cashless System of Commerce 1900 years ago as one in which business would be transacted with a "Mark" and a Number; the Mark will obviously be a Bar Code; the Number will be "666;" the combination of the two, about which you will read in this book, will be an integral part of the "666 System," another term for the World Government System destined to close out this present Age with a 7-year Totalitarian Regime, Daniel's 70th Week. Daniel 9:27.

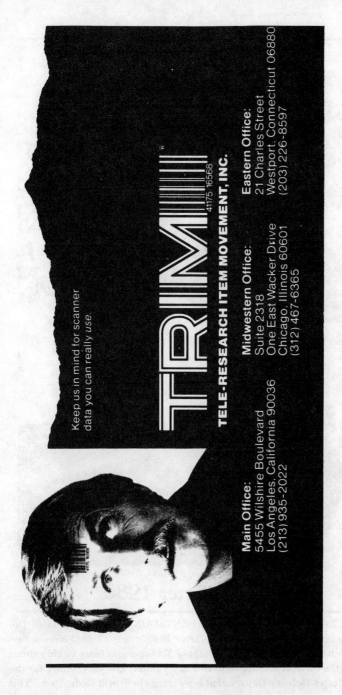

PROPHETICALLY RIGHT ON! "Mark" in forehead.
A very reputable company placed this ad in *Advertising Age Tabloid*, October 20, 1980.

First Quarter 1980

OOPS ... CHANGEOVER AT THE PENTAGON! The United States Defense Department Journal, First Quarter 1980, pages 42 & 43 show a cartoon which depicts the change in Defense Management from an old runner handing the torch of management to a new runner. The new runner for the United States Defense Department is wearing the World Code, "666." This

Defense Management Journal

clearly indicates the United States Defense is now under the influence of the Global Order which will one day consummate in the last One World Government System, whose Politics, Economy, and Religion will be characterized by the Number "666." Revelation 16:18.

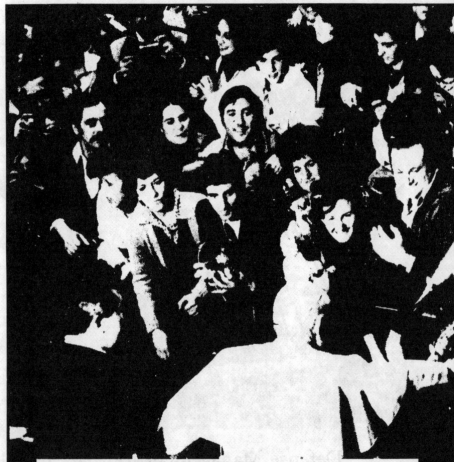

NEW YORK TIMES, February 11, 1979
"Pope John Paul II reaches out to tourists and pilgrims at the Wednesday audience in New York. Tickets are free. Shown in upper right is a blown up version of a ticket which admits one to a papal audience when in Rome." (At lower left is a group of small digits followed by the number "666.")

Sunday, February 11, 1979

Attend a Papal Audience

The World Future Society with headquarters at 4916 St. Elmo Avenue, Washington, D.C., 20014, is a prestigious, nonprofit organization of scientists and scholars concerned with the world's future technologically and sociologically. World Future Society, like other extremely sophisticated groups, promote a "One World" theme. Their logo, when viewed in a mirror, is the Global Identification Number, "666."

Jerusalem Post, November 25, 1980, pictures an advertisement of a Nationwide contest entitled, "Uncover Six Six Six and Win!" Sponsored by the Department of Education and Health Services, it is designed to "educate, prepare, and condition" the Jews to accept these smiling 666's as something not bad, but good! It is the Number of their False Messiah, the antichrist, and his World Government System, which will attempt to exterminate the Jews in the time of Jacob's Trouble, Matthew 24:15; Daniel 9:27; 12:1. It will be Israel's Final Folly. Jesus Christ warned them:

"I am come in my Father's Name, and ye receive me not: if another shall come in his own name, him ye will receive." John 5:43. "Pray for the peace of Jerusalem. They shall prosper that love thee." Psalms 122:6.

TRAVEL WITH ME AS WE DISCUSS:

BAR CODES ARE COMING

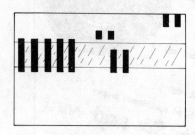

Uncover the "Coded" use of "666" in Bar Codes.

CREDIT CARDS with Bar Codes in them now! Invisible to the naked eye.

Federal Reserve's Debit Cards have Bar Codes; no name or address.

HAND SCANS ARE COMING

"being vigorously marketed." Also the Number in use now!

How a digital watch can be a convenient means of monitoring your whereabouts . . .

That a $3.00 telephone device, the "infinity mike," enables anyone, anywhere in the world to monitor your room without your knowing it.

That a "simple looking" staple machine can pick up and transmit your conversation up to 1½ miles away for recording.

A "camera" from which you can't hide,—underground, in the air, in fog, night, or clouds . . .

And "watch" a piece of luggage as it is electronically monitored from departure to arrival.

As you read, I believe that it will become obvious that the "Control" inherent in this Global (Cashless) Economic System could only be accommodated by 21st Century technology; both of which will combine to produce history's first Worldwide Dictatorship with the audacity to demand, the means to follow up; and the power to receive total allegiance from every person on the earth . . . almost. John Wicklein, in his book, Electronic Nightmare, making no religious application said:

"The new technology makes possible a System in which a national (or international) government could extract from the people all the information it needed to CONTROL THEIR LIVES, and transmit to the people only that information which would aid in that control."[1]

Hopefully, you will discover how these technologies will assist in the control over all "Buying and Selling," and shift the power of all the wealth of the world into the hands of a few who control the System. When all "Buying and Selling" will no longer be accompanied by transfers of money, only electronic pulses juggling account Numbers and "Value Exchanges," then will be brought to pass The New Money System. It will have little to do with Money, it will be operated with "Marks." Those who control the System will have all the Money; the public will have all the "Marks." *And he causeth all to receive a Mark...*" "Charagma in Greek, Impressed Mark; engraving; a stamp containing an encoded message."

"Power (Control) was given him over all kindreds, and tongues and nations. And all that dwell upon the earth shall worship him; whose names are not written in the book of life . . ." Revelation 13:7-8.

NOTES:

1 John Wicklein, *Electronic Nightmare* (New York: The Vicking Press), p. 253.

PROLOGUE

The world's greatest conspiracy is being quietly conducted in the most sacred halls of secular secrecy. While its thrust is Economic, its reach is without limit. No System will escape its mastery, be it Politics or Religion.

The Prime Mover is the most powerful Consortium of financial institutions, captalists, and scientists ever leagued together. Their common purpose is to bring every person, place and thing under their control.

Their applied strategy is by way of IDENTIFICATION. This means of IDENTIFICATION is by way of assignment of MARKS (or bars) for NUMBERS read by machines. (Numbers people can read, Marks they can't ... the name of this game ... Secrecy).

PHASE I began in 1970 with a conscientious effort to "IDENTIFY EVERY ITEM" at the manufacturer's level with a NUMBER "MARKED" on it. A group of Numbers designated by Marks, lines or bars, is called a Bar Code. The Universal Product Code, (Code 39, etc.), and giant computer manufacturers are central to this phase.

PHASE II began in 1973 with an effort to IDENTIFY each PERSON with a Number. The Social Security Numbers when blended with the Universal Numbering System will be converted to "Bars." Initially, this NUMBER will be "Marked" on a Card; (a WORLD-

WIDE MONEY-ID-CARD). Subsequently, according to Bible Prophecy, it will be stamped upon the person it identifies. As the MARK OF IDENTITY on an ITEM is a Bar Code; so the MARK OF IDENTITY on a CARD and later on a person, will be a Bar Code facsimile. The Government, Banks, and Card Companies are central to this phase.

PHASE III is an effort to identify everything in the world whether mobile or stationary;

> If mobile, then how to instantaneously locate it; as a piece of luggage, an expensive race horse, a family car, or a person. Central to this is the Federal Government which has spent ten years in research on "Electronic Identification" at Los Alamos; the Airlines, and private inventors.

> If stationary, as a house, farm, or apartment, the United States Census Department is central to this phase.

The objective of this book is to uncloak the conspiracy, and expose the evils of this System. You can read about the advantages in your local paper. This is the other side of the Cashless Society. More importantly, each development is scrutinized in the light of Bible Prophecy.

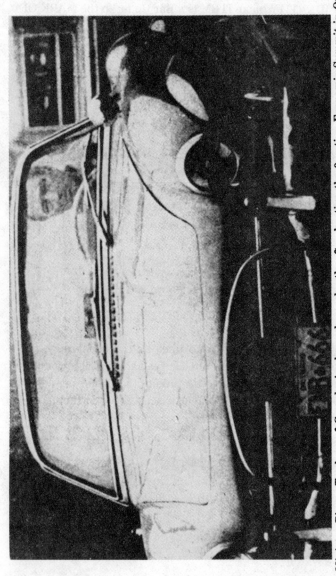

Prime Minister Pierre Trudeau of Canada, is shown here shortly after hosting the 9-nation Economic Summit in Ottawa. The Summit's prime purpose was to discuss ways to "redistribute the wealth of the world." Mr. Trudeau is renowned for his efforts in implementing a World Government movement. HE IS WEARING THE GLOBAL IDENTIFICATION NUMBER, "666" ON THE LICENSE PLATE OF HIS 1959 MERCEDES. Many Federal Government telephones in Canada are prefixed with "666."

TABLE OF CONTENTS

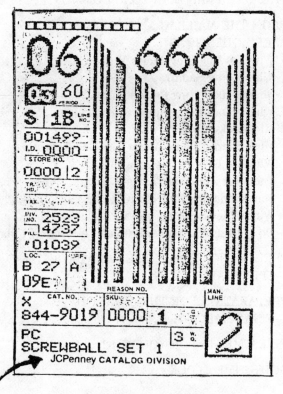

The Bar Code and "666."

CHAPTER I

> *"And he (the last world Dictator) causeth all . . . to receive a Mark." Revelation 13:16.*

THE  AND "666"

In the past my writings have centered on exposing the OPEN usages of "666." This Chapter concentrates on CONCEALED usages of "666" in the end-time Economy. Let him that hath ears hear! Satan's principal activity is deception. (Revelation 20:3&8). The world is about to be deceived.

The Apostle John said: *"Here is WISDOM. Let him that hath UNDERSTANDING count the Number . . . "666."* Obviously, simply counting the Number "666" requires little wisdom. It is so simple a second grader can do it. So there must be a hidden application of "666" which requires **WISDOM** and **UNDERSTANDING** the second grader could not have.

Paul instructed Timothy to *"give attendance to reading;"* which, among other things means, attend your reading sessions with 100% of your mental faculties. Remember, the old adages which illustrate the folly of paying half-attention:

> "When they passed out brains,
> I thought they said trains,
> And I had no place to go;

31

When they passed out noses,
I thought they said roses,
And I ordered a big red one."

This Chapter will require meticulous attention for you to be able to articulate the nuggets of hidden UNDERSTANDING in "counting" this number "666."

——— ——— ———

For about three years I have read and heard that the Universal Product Code incorporated a "coded" usage of "666," in its Bar Code. But, no one seemed to sufficiently "qualify" the claim to my satisfaction. The absence of information initiated a two-year investigation of the subject.

At the outset it became obvious that the "Bar Code" Marking System was first an Identification System, and secondly, an Encodation of these ID Numbers to accomodate "Buying and Selling."

Most disturbing were the inherent ramifications reaching far beyond mere functions in commerce. I could see that the Bar Code technology applied first on products, later on Cards, would be the basic juggernaut in the Cashless Society. And, the merging of Identification with "Buying and Selling" into one electronic pulse, carried with it the awesome means by which a regime could exact total Control over every person's life.

As a student of Bible Prophecy for thirty years, I know just such a totalitarian regime will emerge at the time of the very end of this Age. One of the ways Christians have to identify the lateness of the hour is by studying the economy. When one sees economic activities accelerating so rapidly toward a Cashless System, then look for the usages of the Number "666," for the last Government System to rule the world before the return of Christ to the earth will be Cashless in Commerce, and epitomized by the usage of this Number.

Truth which needs to be reinforced to Christians is that the Holy Spirit still *"TEACHES us ALL things, BRINGS ALL things to our remembrance, GUIDES us into ALL TRUTH, and SHOWS*

32

us things to come." John 14:26; 16:13. Many of the TRUTHS into which He GUIDES us are mysteries of God, *"over which He has made us 'Stewards." I Corinthians 4:1.* As Stewards we are "Caretakers" of Truth ... the Holy Spirit is the Spirit of TRUTH.

Throughout this study which has consisted of many, many hours, the person of the Holy Spirit would BRING to my remembrance that:

1. *"He has hid these things from the WISE and prudent and hast REVEALED them unto babes." Luke 10:21,*

2. *"Not many WISE ... after the flesh are called. I Corinthians 1:26,*

3. *"God hath chosen the FOOLISH things ... to confound the wise." I Corinthians 1:27,*

4. *"Except a man be born again he cannot see ..." John 3:3,*

5. *"... None of the wicked shall understand ..." these things. Daniel 12:10.*

The Cursory Exam

One of the first things I received was a facsimile of a UPC Symbol with a computer language print-out underneath disclosing the use of "666" in the Bar Code. (See title of the chapter). At this juncture it remained a mystery which of the Marks (Bars), if any, represented "666;" or, if the over all Bar Code construction was designed upon these 6's. I received information that leading Supermarket Point of Sale Systems were built to scan Identification Numbers on items consisting of a "6-byte" field using "6 digits" on the left side of the Bar Code, and "6 digits" on the right side.

I proceeded to spend thousands of dollars in researching the origin and development of the Bar Code Marking System. Libraries were searched, new encyclopedias were purchased, titles in industrial publications gleaned, books procured, and finally a brand new Random House Unabridged Dictionary was obtained which was supposed to contain every word in the English language.

Conspicuously missing in all of the afore mentioned was the name per se, and anything about Bar Codes, or Universal Product Code's origin and development. In the Information Society in which we live today where "data moves around the world in the time it takes to snap a shutter,"[1] the absoulte void of information about something so common as the Bar Code had to be more than blatant omission!

Since it obviously was not to be found through normal pursuits, I studied, prayed, and sought for the "hidden wisdom" to understand how to DECODE these "Marking" Symbols. Alas, the Lord quickened to me one day:

> *"Weep not, behold the Lion of the tribe of Juda, the Root*
> *of David, hath prevailed to open the book, and to loose*
> *the seven seals." Revelation 5:5.*

These things had been a closed book since Daniel was commanded to:

> *"Shut up the words, and seal the book even to the time*
> *of the End: Many shall run to and fro, and* **KNOWL-**
> **EDGE** *shall be increased." Daniel 12:4.*

I can now assure you: It is the time of the end; the book is opened, KNOWLEDGE is increased, and God is giving unto His own the *"Spirit of WISDOM and REVELATION in the KNOWL-EDGE of Him, the eyes of our UNDERSTANDING being enlightened." Ephesians 1:17-18.*

BREAKING DOWN
THE UNIVERSAL PRODUCT CODE

The first glimmer in the breaking of the Bar Code Marking System came when I obtained a Set of Bars representing the numbers 0-9. This Optical Character Recognition (OCR) B font identified "Bars" (Lines or Marks) for Numbers. With this conversion chart of "Bars for Numbers" it became apparent that **two uniform lines** were being used to depict the Number 6 in the Universal Product Code's most commonly used Bar Code. See Figure 1, 2&3.

FIGURE 1

All Marks (Bars) in the Symbol are identified by Numbers at the bottom, except three sets of "two uniform Bars" which appear identical to "6."

FIGURE 2

The only Marks unidentified by Numbers in this basic UPC DESIGN are shown isolated in Positions 1,2, and 3.

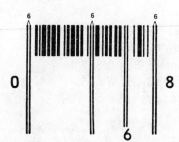

FIGURE 3

A visual inspection of the three "always unidentified Bars" compared to the Bar UPC identifies as "6" isolated.

35

From Figures 1, 2, and 3, one can see that this recent UPC Design has all Marks identified with respective Numbers, except in three places which I have designated Positions #1, #2, and #3. Each unidentified Bar consists of two uniform Marks, whose construction is identified elsewhere in this Symbol as "6."

From the cursory inspection it became obvious that the same Bar which represents "6" in the body of the Symbol is used three times to form a framework for the Design.

There was still much, so much to be understood. During my research, I received a letter from a man I did not know, and from whom I had never heard. It read:

"Dear Mary,

Please listen to this tape, and follow on the papers with the tape. **God gave me the interpretation of the lines (Bars) in the UPC Mark so I could give them to you, because you have the means of getting this out to the people, and because you have asked it of God.**

I love you Mary, as a sister in the Lord, and for the work you have done in your book. What is on this tape will greatly add to the proofs and truths of your book.

Please, Mary, in Jesus name I ask, for the sake of all the souls that will be won to the Kingdom of God through the message on this tape, get the message out to the people."

Your brother in the Lord,
John H. Shepherd
Route 2, Box 268AA
Martinsburg, WV 25401
1-304-274-1959

I looked at the paper John sent. I began to listen to the tape. Like a flash of lightning I SAW IT. The Code WAS BROKEN! It was as easy to see as the sun on a clear day.

I acknowledged that this had not come out of the libraries, encyclopedias, or electronic publications, but the *Lion of the tribe of Juda had prevailed!* The book had been opened! Knowledge had been increased! the TIME of the END was upon us. I paused in the presence of the ONE who came ***"declaring the END from the beginning and from ancient times the things which are not yet done,"*** *((Isaiah 46:10)* and worshipped HIM *"which was, and is, and is to come," (Revelation 4:8)*, and whose coming back to earth is nigh, even at the door.

I praised Him for my brother John, whose face I had never seen, but through whom I beleive God spoke a long prayed-for understanding of the mechanics designed in the last Global Economic System where business will be transacted using a "Mark" in which **wisdom and knowledge will be required to "count" the Number "666."**

Some 1900 years ago, God chose to use an Apostle whose name was John to prophecy that the last "Buying and Selling" System of this World Order would be conducted with a "Mark." In 1981, God chose to use another man whose name is John to interpret the lines in the "Mark." Whoever said God is dead should recant. He's alive! and *"revealeth His secret unto His servants . . .!" Amos 3:7.*

I feel impressed of the Lord to present John's material here as I received it. His original charts have been left intact. A commercial artist improved upon their appearance only for the book. I will follow this section with the Industry's explanation of the Symbols.

How To Identify "666" In All UPC Symbols
by John H. Shepherd

"Mary, god spoke these things to my heart the evening of August 31, 1981." For simplicity's sake, and so as not to lose you, I am going to teach that there are three Sets of Marks (Bars) for the Numbers from 0 through 9, but for a grand total of only 25. However, only 21 DIFFERENT BARS are used. (See explanation at the close of this section.) You can "decode" each UPC Symbol with these three Sets.

Sets

FIGURE 4

Set #1 is designated by the number 1
Set #2 is designated by the number 2
Set #3 is designated by the number 3

39

FIGURE 5

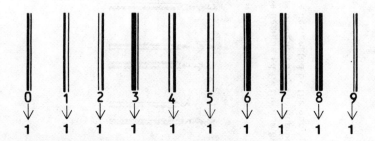

Set #1 isolated

FIGURE 6

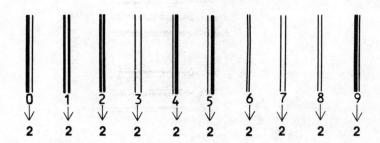

Set #2 isolated

FIGURE 7

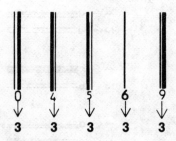

Set #3 isolated

FIGURE 8

Side A | Design #1 | Side B

Figure 8 is a copy of what I am calling Design #1, the most frequently used UPC Symbol. Some absolutes governing its construction are:

1. The only Marks in Design #1 unidentified by Numbers beneath will always be constructed as three 6's from Set 2.

2. This DESIGN is always divided into two sides, separated in the middle, and enclosed on both ends by "Uniform Marks" constructed as 6-6-6 from Set 2. Look at the Marks for 6, Set 2.

3. Ten bold Numbers are always printed beneath in this DESIGN.

4. Only Marks for Set 1 and Set 2 are used in this DESIGN.

5. The ten bold Numbers appear five on either side; as here, 11230 on Side A, and 80101 on Side B.

6. Side A will always use Marks from Set 1; Side B from Set 2. To illustrate this, see Figures 9 and 10.

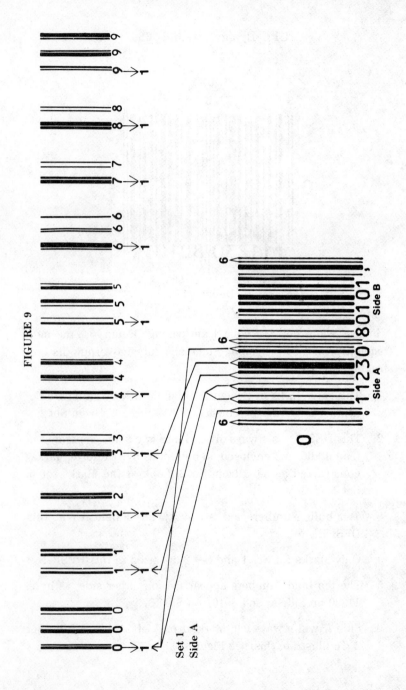

FIGURE 9

Design #1, Side A Explained

Design #1 is the most commonly used UPC Symbol. Here Side A is explained. Lines are drawn from Side A to indicate these Marks are taken from Set 1, (and Side B from Set 2.).

Side A ALWAYS uses Marks from Set 1 when ten bold Numbers appear beneath Symbol Code, five on either side, which indicate this is UPC DESIGN #1.

(There are 6 Bars on either side, the 5 bold Numbers printed on the left identify the manufacturer; the small 0 is a System Number. The five bold Numbers on the right identify the product, and the small 5 is another coincidental Number ... it must have six on either side.)

Please follow lines drawn from DESIGN to Marks in Set 1 representing same Numbers. You must "see" this to understand how to "decode" the Symbols.

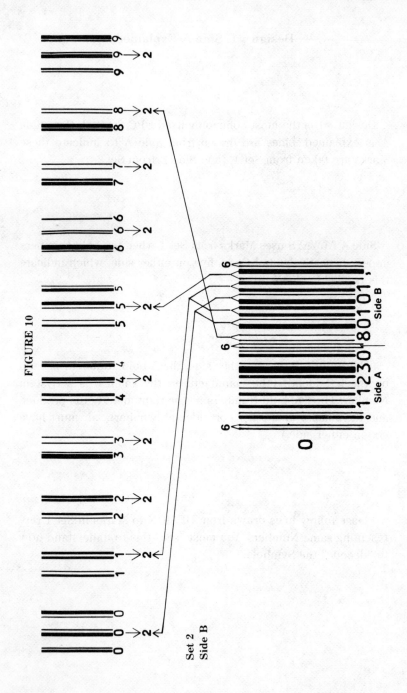

FIGURE 10

44

Design #1, Side B Explained

Side B ALWAYS uses Marks from Set 2 when ten bold Numbers appear beneath Code, five on either side, which indicate this is UPC DESIGN #1. Follow lines from DESIGN to Marks in Set 2 presenting same Numbers. The three only unidentified Bars are Marks using construction of "666."

FIGURE 11

MADE IN THAILAND

0   6

70555 00145

Side A   Side B

6

Another UPC Design #1

Ten bold Numbers are at the bottom, five on either side; Numbers on Side A are represented by Marks from Set 1; Numbers from Side B are represented by Marks from Set 2. NOTE THE 6 ON THE RIGHT SIDE REPRESENTS THE NEXT-TO-LAST CHARACTER DEPICTING 6; (IT APPEARS JUST AS LAST CHARACTER DEPICTING UNIDENTIFIED 6): but, it has to do with a check Number and is not part of the unidentified Code of Bars depicted as "6-6-6." (Anytime the Number 6 is printed (identified) anywhere in the body of the Symbol, it has nothing to do with the three unidentified Bars forming the framework.)

I recommend that you go now to your shelves, take out the canned goods, and other items, and begin "decoding" all the UPC DESIGNS #1, **WHICH PRINT TEN BOLD NUMBERS AT THE BOTTOM** of the Symbol indicating it is DESIGN #1. **You will find the Code in every Symbol!**

UPC Design #2, and "666"

Since one basic design could possibly be cracked, there had to be others to assure its continued secrecy to the general public. We shall examine the second most commonly used UPC Symbol which has SIX (not ten) bold Numbers, printed beneath the Symbol. This is exactly one-half of DESIGN #1, or one Side. It has six Bars plus the three frame Bars. These appear on general grocery items also. See Figure 12.

FIGURE 12

UPC DESIGN #2 is the second most commonly seen UPC DESIGN. All Bars identified by Numbers beneath Symbol except three.

Refer back to Figures 9 and 10 to observe the single Mark for 6 from Set 3, which is used here to represent the second 6 in "666."

The three "Unidentified Bars" isolated. The Code "666" is in a different configuration in this DESIGN.

UPC Design #2

FIGURE 13

Each Bar identified by Numbers beneath from sets noted above.

Bars are used from all three sets in DESIGN #2. The Bars which are identified by the six bold Numbers beneath are taken from Sets 1,2 and 3 as shown in Figure 13.

The 6 bold Numbers printed beneath the Symbol have nothing to do with the unidentified Bars, the framework of the Symbol.

At left in Figure 13, note the use of the two 8's; neither is alike; also two 0's, neither is represented by the same Marks. Mass confusion would ensue in attempting to break this Code were it not for DIVINE WISDOM.

FIGURE 14

Side A   Side B   Side C

UPC Design #1 Extended

This Symbol is found on magazines and books. It is basically the same as Figure 8, but with an extension.

The Bars used in Side A are taken from Set 1; Side B from Set 2.

The extension in this example "9066" uses Marks from all three sets, but has nothing to do with the Coded use of "666" in the body of the Symbol.

47

UPC Design #1 - Hyphenated, and "666"

FIGURE 15

Patent medicines have ten bold Numbers which are hyphenated and appear in groups of 4,4 and 2; (instead of 5 and 5). Don't let this confuse you; 00890 is Side A; 91303 is Side B. Side A uses Marks from Set 1; Side B from Set 2. The Coded use of "666" is just as in DESIGN #1.

UPC Design #2
(Without Numbers)
Supermarket Shelf
Bar Codes and "666"

FIGURE 16

This information came off Supermarket Shelves! Both Sets of Bar Codes with no Numbers printed underneath use the basic construction as shown in Figures 12 and 13.

The Marks are actually identified by numbers on the far left side.

Here "085-008" and "085-128" are depicted by Bars used from all three Sets. THE CODED USE OF "666" IS EVEN TACKED ON THE SHELVES of the Supermarkets!

IN CONCLUSION
John H. Shepherd

"The computer knows the difference in UPC DESIGNS. Actually, the Lord showed me that there are only two real sets of Marks; one for DESIGN #1 which consists of the first two Sets, for a total of 20 Marks. The other Set of Marks for DESIGN #2 thusly:

DESIGN #1 will never use any of Set 3 in Figure 4; 0,4,5,6, or 9.

DESIGN #2 will never use the following from Set 2; 0,4,5, and 9.

These Bars are taken from Set 2 to represent other Numbers in Set 3.

SET #2		SET #3
0 .... becomes		.5
5 .... becomes		.0
4 .... becomes		.9
9 .... becomes		.4

"So, Set 3 is made up by using some of Set 2 assigning different Numbers to same Bars. I say again, there are not three Sets. There are two Sets for DESIGN #1; a variation of these for DESIGN #2. THE ONLY NUMBER FOR WHICH THREE DIFFERENT BARS EXIST IS THE NUMBER "6." Is it not strange the only Number represented with 3 different Bars is 6, "6-6-6?" Six from Set 3 is really ½ of Bar 6 in Set 2, or one-half of the two uniform lines, as DESIGN #2 IS EXACTLY ½ OF DESIGN #1-EVEN TO HALFING THE CENTER BAR FOR 6.

"Mary, the Lord showed me that there are many Bar Codes, several UPC DESIGNS, but only two Primary UPC DESIGNS being used in Super Markets now. Sometimes these may have extensions, hyphenations, or some other form of variations; but, the Code concealing the use of "666" will be in both of the two configurations as shown earlier.

"You will find a little study of the Marks will enable you to clearly see the 'neatly planned' deceit in causing people to unknowingly 'Buy and Sell' with a "Mark" in which is concealed the use of this Number which the Prophet John said would require Wisdom and Understanding to count, '666.' "

End

VERIFICATION OR QUALIFICATION

While John professes to have received all this via Divine Revelation from the Holy Spirit, in one evening, the same Holy Spirit impressed me to continue my study in the technical area, and present my findings, the result of many weeks of effort.

In the official brochure entitled, "About The Universal Product Code" is found the following statements:

Purposes of the UPC

"The UPC can be used as a Common Identification System ..."

Source Symbol-Marking

"The economic success ... depends on the agreement of manufacturers to MARK the CODE NUMBER and its companion Symbol on each consumer package."

Definition of the UPC

"The UPC should be viewed as having two related parts: first, a CODE or NUMBERING SYSTEM that is INTENDED to IDENTIFY EVERY ITEM SOLD by retailers; second, a 'machine readable representation' (Symbol) ..."

The brochure hails the "Universal Product Code and Symbol" as "perhaps two of the most significant achievements of the decade ..."

Note comparison in terminology in this brochure, and in Revelation 13:16-18. John, the Revelator, wrote that people would in the end-time economy be required to receive a Mark which would identify them for the purpose of "Buying and Selling." The UPC System first IDENTIFIES; (and using Bible terminology), then "MARKS the CODE NUMBER ... on each ... package," and finally intends "to IDENTIFY EVERY ITEM SOLD." When every item manufactured can be IDENTIFIED, Bought and Sold, with a "Coded" Number, what a small matter for an amplified System to IDENTIFY every person with similar technology.

FIGURE 17

= 12345-67890
(Note: First 5 digits assigned by UPCC, Inc.; second 5 by manufacturer)

A blown-up version of the UPC Symbol explained in official brochure of the Uniform Product Code Council, Inc. I have identified the Bars above the Symbol with Sets used by John H. Shepherd. Side A is from Set 1, Side B is from Set 2. Three positions are occupied by unidentified Bars, I am identifying as 6's.

The Industry Says . . .

Mr. Richard J. Mindlin, Executive Vice-President of the Uniform Product Code Council, Inc., who has been very helpful in promptly supplying us with resource material, wrote in response to our inquiry:

"There are no unidentified characters in the Symbol, as each Encodation serves either as *data characters* or for information to indicate to the scanner to *start or stop* reading. These START and STOP Characters are not the same as the ENCODATION for the digit 6."

I preceived that wisdom was to delineate the difference in the Encodation of Data Characters Bars, particularly of the Digit "6" used within the Symbol, and the Encodation of Information Bars used as Start and Stop Characters which "frame" the Symbol.

The "difference" had already sent me probing into the furthermost limits of "Symbol Construction." Hopefully I can reduce many hours of intricate technical details to a brief readable synopsis.

FIGURE 17A

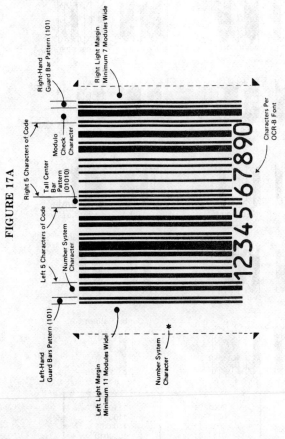

Left-Hand
Guard Bars Pattern (101)

Left 5 Characters of Code

Number System
Character

Tall Center
Bar Pattern
(01010)

Right 5 Characters of Code

Modulo
Check
Character

Right-Hand
Guard Bar Pattern (101)

Right Light Margin
Minimum 7 Modules Wide

Characters Per
OCR-B Font

Left Light Margin
Minimum 11 Modules Wide

Number System
Character

*

UPC Standard Symbol (Version A)

From a little study of the Standard UPC Symbol, Version A, it can be seen that the three always unidentified Bars are called Leftand Right Guard Bars and Center Bar Patterns whose encodings are designed differently from Data Character Bars. Herein lies the "invisible" difference. Each Number in the UPC Symbol is encoded as two light spaces and two dark bars. Each Number is further divided into seven equal data elements called modules. See Figure 18.

xxxxxxxxxxxxxxxxxxxxxxxxxxxxxxxxxxxxxxxxxxxxxxxxxxxxxxxxxxxxxxxxxxxxxxxxxxxxu

FIGURE 19

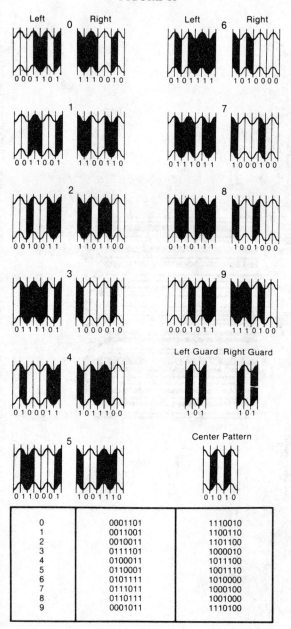

0	0001101	1110010
1	0011001	1100110
2	0010011	1101100
3	0111101	1000010
4	0100011	1011100
5	0110001	1001110
6	0101111	1010000
7	0111011	1000100
8	0110111	1001000
9	0001011	1110100

54

UPC Standard Symbol, Version A Encoding for entire Set. From NCR Reference Library NCR 225/726 Information. Pages 7 & 8.

Figure 19

- Note the difference in 7-Module Encodation for Data Characters, and 3 and 5-Module Encodation for Left, Right and Center Bar Patterns.

- Left, Right, and Center Bars are designated by Function only (not by digit) with Encodation determining construction.

- The Encodation for Left, Right, and Center Bars are the only visible components of the digit "6," 101, and 01010.

- It is my opinion that the "Information" Bars (encoded differently from Data Characters) are 3 and 5-Module 6's, and this alone differentiates them from a 7-Module Data Character 6. (The Left and Right Sets are the same as John Shepherd's Sets 1 and 2. This is confirmed with a brief visual comparison).

FIGURE 18

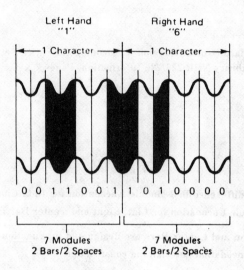

Symbol Data Character (Digit) Decoding from NCR Reference Library, NCR 255/726 System Inforamtion, Page 6.

• Note each Number (Data Character) encoded as a Bar in the Symbol is represented by a binary Code using a combination of 0 and 1 to denote all Numbers. The Bars are designated as 1, the light spaces as 0.

• The Number 1 (as shown above) when used as a Data Character is encoded as 0011001.

• The "Number 6" (as shown above) WHEN USED AS A DATA CHARACTER is encoded as 1010000. NOTE THE ONLY VISIBLE MODULES OF "6" are the Encodation "101."

FIGURE 20

0

453110

UPC Version E (Design #2)

0	0001101	0100111
1	0011001	0110011
2	0010011	0011011
3	0111101	0100001
4	0100011	0011101
5	0110001	0111001
6	0101111	0000101
7	0111011	0010001
8	0110111	0001001
9	0001011	0010111

UPC Symbol Version E Encoding

This is much like the first half of Version A. The 6-digit Code, when entered in the System, becomes a 10-digit Code. The Right Guard Bars use a 6-Module Encodation "010101" for the extra dark Bar.

In studying the differences in the encoding of Bars for Version A versus Bars for Version E, I found:

1. Using John's Conversion Chart, 0 of Set 2 becomes 5 of set 3; etc. See page 45.

2. Set 1 (Left Characters) and Set 2 (Right Characters) began encoding with 0's. Compare with Figure 19.

Why All the Sixes?

After many hours of study, I concluded that when "6" is used as a "Data Character," it is a 7-module "6"; when used as a "Start and Stop Character," it is a 3 or 5-module "6." Now to paraphrase:

> "The question comes to me,
> As I gaze at prophecy,
> Why all the Sixes?"

There are 18 other Bar Codes from whose construction the Guard Bars could have borrowed. Why "6?" Why "6" Bars on the Left Side, and "6" Bars on the Right Side of the Standard Version Symbol? Why "6" Bars in the second most commonly used Symbol E? Why is the entire Item Number Field a "6-Byte" Record Identification? Why are there "6" different versions of the UPC codes?

Computer technicians say, "6" is the perfect computer number." Apple Computer Inc. celebrated the reality of this when they introduced their first 200 Apple I units to be "retailed for $666.66." Wall Street Journal, 11-11-81.

Prophecy students know that "6's" are among the secrets of the economy destined to close out this Age. They also know that it will take wisdom and understanding to "compute" them.

Ah, John, that is the understatement of the Age ... considerably more than a second grader could "count."

Standard Formats of Bar Codes

Codabar

3 1177 00345 6570

CODE 39

Interleaved Two of Five

535 0458 4422

UPC Version E

:115476

UPC Version A

015400 852654

- Only the last two are UPC Versions). "Code 39" encodes numbers plus alphabetic characters.

- Encodations other than Bar Codes are machine readable. OCR is an encoding human and machine readable, and used by retail chains. The OCR Wands are passed over information. Wands have a 30% "No Read" on first pass, and a 1% misread. With a little extra ink or dirt the Wand reads an F for an E.

- Bar Code Encodations are scanned from 20 to 1000 times per second and efficiency and accuracy are trademarks of Bar Code Encodation, versus say "human readable" Encodations.

Printability Gage

A ||||| ≡ A'
B ||||| ≡ B'
C ||||| ≡ C'
D ||||| ≡ D'
E ||||| ≡ E'
F ||||| ≡ F'
G ||||| ≡ G'
H ||||| ≡ H'
I ■ ■ I'
J ■ ■ J'
K ■ ■ K'

Students of prophecy have speculated on the reasons for additional sections of lines seen with some Bar Codes, particularly of F and H appearing on a few. In the absence of easily available information, we have conjectured it could be F for forehead, and H for hand. There is enough accurate information pointing to fulfillment of Bible Prophecy for any intelligent person to know the hour is late. The F and H are used to establish a rating of printability.

Bar Codes Are International

I have spent my lifetime at the frontiers of new thought in several disciplines, but never have I perceived a revelation so exciting as the one foretold by John 1900 years ago. This fisherman prophesied that the economy of the end of this Age would be conducted not with "Money" but with "Marks;" "Marks" on people, in association with the use of "666." Now in 1982, we are watching the evolution of this "Marking System." First begun in the decade of the 70's, in the United States on manufactured goods, it is now being implemented internationally in the decade of the 80's.

The Sunday Post, March 8, 1981, Glasgow, Scotland

Secret Code In The Supermarket

**EAN Symbol Used
In the United Kingdom**

"Little black lines and numbers are now on over 4000 items in shops and supermarkets.

It's the beginning of a new method of shopping, which will soon be familiar to every housewife in the land.

Here's how the system works.

The lines are known as 'bar code.'

When a customer reaches the cash register, the assistant will no longer ring up the price on the item's label — for there won't be a price on the label!

Instead, she'll draw a light-sensitive pen across the bar code.

The code is automatically sent into a computer, which recognizes the pattern of bars, and identifies the purchase — a 4 oz. tin of beans, or whatever.

The computer then flashes the price, which is stored in its memory, on to the cash register display, and the cash register gives a printed receipt, listing each item and its price, which the customer can still check.

It means each item won't be individually priced, though the price will be clearly displayed on the shelf.

The numbers beside the bar code give the country of manufacture, maker's name, and the particular item — e.g., an 8 oz. can of peas, a 1 litre bottle of squash, & etc.

In short, the bar code clearly identifies each product for the computer — and the computer does the rest.

Advantages are, it speeds up check-out queues, rules out mistakes at the check-out, tells a shop what it's selling and what it's running out of, and saves individual pricing.

At the moment, only six shops in Britain are actually using the system, all in England.

But within a few years it's likely every large store in the country will have changed to the new system.''

From this article let us notice:

1. This Symbol is NOT called the Universal Product Code. This is too American sounding. Each area of the world will lend its distinctive designation. In Europe, it is called EAN, European Article Numbers. The Construction of the EAN Symbol is slightly different from the UPC Design #1. Each Bar in the EAN Symbol is identified by the Number it represents; (six on either side; twelve bold Numbers) except, the Left, Right and Center Bars. TWO UNIFORM MARKS on the Right Side identify "6" for us. The Encodation of the EAN is different so that the computer can readily identify the manufacturer's continent.
2. "The Bar Code CLEARLY IDENTIFIES EACH PRODUCT for the computer."
3. "Within a few years" the new System will be throughout the country.
4. "Advantages are, it speeds up check-out queues, RULES OUT MISTAKES at the checkout ..."

The UPC Scam

Note #3 ... "It rules out mistakes at the check-out ..." This is an important part of the "misinformation" (indoctrination) campaign fed to the public. Let us analyze the fallacy of this "advantage" being used to promote the System.

Fresh meats and produce do not lend themselves to Bar Code Symbols being attached to the items per se. As a result, a problem of great magnitude has already surfaced. Quoting from the Montgomery Advertiser, October 23, 1981:

"PRICE TAG SWITCH NEWEST ELECTRONIC GAME IN CITY STORES ... The supermarket cashier did not notice the $7 package of meat she was ringing up registered as a 64-cent bunch of bananas on her electronic cash register. Another cashier who happened to be facing the machine noticed it, however. As the two shoppers with the cheap meat walked toward the exit, the second cashier called the manager. The manager stopped the two women, and told them to wait while he called the police. They bolted, and left their shopping cart. In the cart was more than $80 worth of meat. They had paid $17 for it. This happened at a Montgomery grocery store earlier this week, authorities said. The two shoppers got away ... Of more concern to authorities is the method of the attempted theft — the computer-coded price tags were replaced or switched on the expensive meat, and the price of the meat was registered as that of the less expensive item. This is a scam. It's brand new to Montgomery, said Bob Bryant of District Attorney Jimmy Evans' office. Police and the district attorney's office are investigating the thefts."

Another classic example of Society paying for their sins — everyone of them. Not only monetarily, but with more far reaching ramifications. This will result in the necessity of removing the prices from the items which our eyes can read; a terrible inconvenience, plus paying inspectors or cashiers to watch each item scanned ... adding personnel ... which brings us back to square one. This not only negates the System's claim that it is faster, more accurate, and less expensive, but points up the most volatile problem of any System ever yet devised. Logic teaches us that there could never be a System as fast, efficient and fool proof as a check-out clerk who punches the price WHILE seeing and feeling "bananas are PRODUCE, not MEAT."

The Bar Code System Test

Note #2 ... 'The Bar Code CLEARLY IDENTIFIES EACH PRODUCT for the computer." There are hundreds of products to each individual in the world. For example, you walk into the Supermarket and there may be only twenty people in there, but there are thousands of products. Right?

At the heart of the "Marking" System is this: If a National or International System can IDENTIFY every little article with a Bar Code, it will be a MORE THAN ADEQUATELY TESTED SYSTEM WHEN IT WILL BE CALLED UPON TO IDENTIFY WITH A BAR CODE, EVERY INDIVIDUAL.

Bar Codes—From Labels to Products

Already the shift is on to place the Bar Code "Marks" on all goods, not just on labels. The United States, Japan, Canada, and Europe are moving toward the "Mark" being manufactured in the article per se, as on the dress material, pant fabric, etc., so that to remove it would deface them. The major deterrent is some material does not lend itself to this ... YET.

> "If you have a new car, look under the hood. You will see lots of Bar Code Symbols ... the Federal Government is working on a program to apply Bar Codes to just about everything it purchases — hundreds of thousands of items, ... The Bar Code concept has been in

use at the retail level since the late '70's, but is just beginning to make an impact," states Mr. Milton Field, Marketing Services Manager, Matthews International, Pittsburgh Press, June 21, 1981.

The advantages of all articles being Marked are enormous in the eyes of this Consortium. When the System is fully functional, and all purchases are made via Electronic Funds Tranafer (The Cashless Society), it can be determined in a moment of time if one's clothes, furniture, or automobile has been purchased by the person who purports to own them, or if not, by whom. To remove the Bar Code from say, a lawn mower is an admission of guilt. The Bar Code will identify the product from manufacturer to distributor to retailer to consumer. With this one feature of this "Marking System," thefts, burglaries, hold-ups, and robberies could virtually be eliminated. Expect bewildered Law Enforcement Officials to hail this as the most ingenious deterrent to crime ever conceived. Even Dick Tracy continues to stay just ahead of the times. See illustration.

Dick Tracy

Reprinted by permission of the Chicago Tribune—New York News Syndicate, Inc.

The Invisible Bar Code

It is highly possible that the Supermarket "SCAM" Game will be rectified by the use of a Laser Gun which will imprint the meats and produce with invisible Bar Codes. Sophisticated scanning devices are already using an "omnidirectional" pattern which would be able to seek the Bar Code out. When this step is implemented, it could be the "salvation" of Supermarket EFT.

Expect Bar Codes to go "underground" only as it appears advantageous to the System. Before the requirement to insert the "Marks" on people, Bar Codes will become invisible. All research done in this vein involving persons has used techniques which appear invisible to the unaided eye. A good historical treatment of this section can be found in the book, *WHEN YOUR MONEY FAILS*.

Radiation Caution Ignored

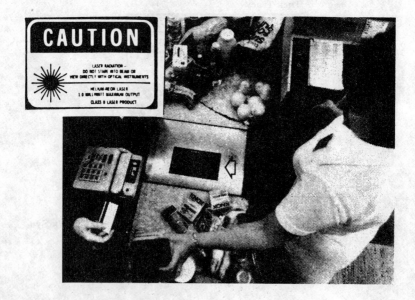

Inherent within this System (as all new Systems) are many unknowns, not the least of which concern continued exposure to Laser Radiation.

The Supermarket Scanner does a "wrap-around job," so that no UPC Symbol must be placed directly above the beam ... its rays spread out in every direction. Perhaps few clerks and fewer customers ever read the Caution Label which the manufacturer affixes just beneath the glass plate ... "LASER RADIATION."

Listed among the advantages in one brochure advertising their Laser Scanner is:

"Lasers can read Bar Codes under plastic and glass from several inches to several feet away."

If Laser Beams can reach Bar Codes "several feet away" with sufficient concentration to read the small Symbols, radiation is also reaching out to clerks and customers in that same intensity to "several feet away," and in less "stimulated emissions" over greater areas.

The check-out girls will be the first to know what constant exposure to this Laser Radiation does to the body. But, like lead and asbestos poisoning, it could take a few years.

Certainly, the manufacturers of Scanning Equipment obviously believe what they state that the radiation is insignificant. Thirty years ago X-Ray Manufacturers were making similar claims about their machines. Twenty years later, sales of those same machines were accompanied by installation procedures calling for 12″ of solid steel insulation in clinic and hospital settings to protect those constantly exposed in the operation. These safe-guards came too late for many technicians and physicians. My own husband, a physician, developed leukemia after 25 years of exposure from inadequately protected X-Rays in his private office. The disease was fatal.

The moral here is simple. Why discard something clean, time tested, and efficient for a Pig in a Poke?

What Shall We Do Then?

The Consortium would have never dared inquire of the public if they wanted such a System in the Supermarkets, which is the basic testing ground for Bar Codes. I view it no less than an outright insult to consumer intelligence. Our eyes can adequately IDENTIFY a can of coffee, and why can't the checker punch in the price on a cash register? Who minds the additional second it takes as opposed to scanning? No consumer would have ever opted to pay for the groceries plus the expensive new scanning check-out lanes with their potentially hazardous radiation.

However, we in the United States are already so deeply entrenched, and leading the way in this Electronic Funds Transfer, that it seems futile to encourage anyone to resist it. To boycott products already "Marked" with Bar Codes would cause one to have to revert to a lifestyle of a century ago. People far and near have enthusiastically written to us about their absolute refusal to use Cards with "666" embossed on the front, and in this they still had a choice. Who among us can, however, with the same resolve, refuse to purchase products on which are stamped the UPC Mark which I believe incorporates the "Coded" use of "666," and certainly is structured on 6's; 6-byte, 6 left bars, 6 right bars.

There are two sides to this record. One is to "Mark" every product with all information necessary to identify, transfer, buy or sell it via a Bar Code. This is virtually accomplished; and, considering millions of dollars have been spent by innocent entrepreneurs on equipment to accomodate this Sytem, any opposition to it, in the absence of God, would make only minor waves. However, Side One has not been completed. Consider:

> "Only one in ten of America's food stores has moved into the fast lane of the checkout counters, using optical scanners to read the Universal Product Code printed on packaged groceries. One reason for delay by some is the cost—as much as $125,000 for instal-

lation in a four-lane store." The Montgomery Advertiser, October 9, 1981.

Your Attention Please!

Please pray before you act on the things I am about to discuss.
The time has come when Christians have to be "wise as serpents,
but harmless as doves." Many have ZEAL, but little KNOWLEDGE,
and these hurt the cause of Christ.

For example, one reader in Denver purchased a book in a Supermarket. The book contained references about the inherent evils
of the Scanning System begun in Supermarkets. The person believed the information in the book, took the book to the Supermarket from which she made the purchase, and caused such a
disturbance that the Manager banned the book, not the Scanning
Devices. The person intended well, but she caused many to be
denied the privilege of buying the book, and reduced the profits
the Christian Distributor could have made on the sale of it. Only
Satan benefited.

PLEASE DO NOT DECIDE ON ANY COURSE OF ACTION UN-
TIL YOU READ THE REMAINDER OF THE BOOK. Much more
follows ...

After reading Chapter II, your understanding will be deepened.
You will see that this is just One Segment of One Industry. Beyond
this is the Banking Industry, the Credit Card Companies, the Computer Manufacturers, the Scientists, and the Politicians who say
that the salvation of mankind is dependent upon a New International Economic Order whose chief thrust is a Cashless System.

Now consider these things:

When a scanner takes the price from the UPC on the article;
(that is, the cashier doesn't punch in the cost); you are using the
Bar Code "Mark" upon products with which to buy; **obviously an
imminent portent of the Mark of the Beast.**

Where cashiers still punch in the price of the product on a cash register; you are only buying a product with a Bar Code Mark "on it," but you are not buying "with it."

The flip side of the record is different. Only the prelude has been played. The public is just beginning to dance to its music. Side Two is to "Mark" all Cards with "womb to tomb" information necessary to IDENTIFY the person, so that he may be "ENTITLED" to have transferred to him the "Marked" products, via Electronic Funds Transfer; thus "Buying and Selling" with a "Mark." (Buying implies Selling: merchants sells, public buys = one transaction). The key is YOU and YOUR CARD. (The power of resistance to the entire Cashless System lies in your refusing CARDS! Pay with Cash and Checks as long as possible).

"The deadline for converting ALL U.S. BANK CARDS to the magnetic tape is March 1982." (Business Week, February 23, 1981, p.107). After this date, all information pertinent to financial transactions will be micro-encoded in the discretionary data track of the mag stripe. Micro-encodations on mag stripes appear under magnification much like the encodations on Bar Codes — both look to the untrained eye as "Marks." See Figures 26 and 27.

FIGURE 26

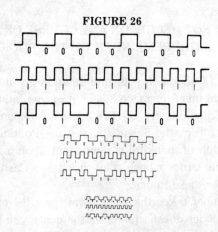

- **Micro-encodation of a Magnetic Stripe using different magnifications. Wait! These would "qualify" as "Marks" too, and they are on Cards . . . read about them in Chapter II.**

70

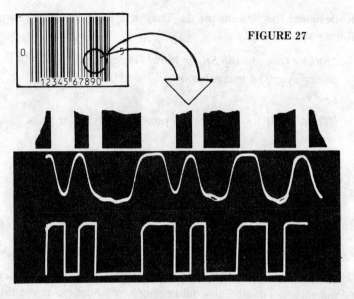

FIGURE 27

- A magnified section of the UPC Symbol. Note the Light Spaces are more reflective than the Dark Bars. When the Symbol is scanned by a Laser, the optical pattern is converted to an electrical signal (analog), which is converted to a digital signal; then decoded by a microprocessor.

- If a child were to go the chalk board and draw these, I believe they would "qualify" as "Marks."

As you read the next Chapter, I believe that you will agree that soon each individual in the world must be identified with the same kind of devices, scanned by the same kind of equipment, to accomplish the ultimate objective of the Cashless System ... the ELIMINATION OF THE CASH REGISTER. Commerce is designed soon to be conducted by an "electronic transaction," at which time an "Exchange of Value" will take place.

The Point of Sale (POS) Terminals, (Value-Exchange Registers) will be doing a juggling act with "Values" and Account Numbers; the latter being represented by "Marks" or "Bars" in a Bar Code. There will be no need for Cash Registers — there will be no cash. All the real money (not fiat money) will be controlled by those who designed the System for us. They will have the Money; we will have the "Marks."

> *"But he (the coming Super World Dictator) shall have power over the treasures of gold and silver." Daniel 11:43.*

"Then shall be brought to pass the saying that is written:"
Money, like freedom and privacy, will have come to pass, it didn't come to stay.

Pray

I hope that you have "hung" in here throughout this Chapter. As Paul said to Timothy, it would require "attendance" in reading to have done so. But, Oh! What a small price to pay for this "understanding" in comparison to the time some few of us have spent in order to present it to you "DECODED." It may necessitate your buying a magnifying glass with a handle to more easily discern the Bars. My own cost $10.00 and was purchased at an Optometry Shop. But, KNOWLEDGE AT ANY PRICE IS A BARGAIN ... for the lack of it, God said, *"MY PEOPLE ARE DESTROYED:"* for the rejection of it, God said, *"I WILL REJECT THEE!"* Hosea 4:6 Now, to whom much is given, much is required! My responsibility is to write it; yours is to do as God directs you!

Now I appeal to all Christians, PRAY. PRAY for the many astute business and professional men who make up much of the management of the Industries promoting the Cashless System, (Electronic Funds Transfer), of which the Supermarket "Marking" System is just one facet. I would believe most of these are hard working men of high integrity. Most know little or nothing about Bible Prophecy. Perhaps only a handful of engineers are aware of the "Marking" System being built upon 6's, or that the last Economic System of this Age will be conducted with "Marks." All of these are people God loves, and for whom Christ died.

PRAY that they may understand that when this System is fully implemented, it will be seized by a World Dictator, empowered by Satan, who will cause all ... *to receive a "Mark"* (stamp of an encoded message) *in their right hand or in their forehead; Revelation 13:16, and that no person may "Buy or Sell" except he/she has it; Revelation 13:16-17.* And because of this, millions of souls will be damned. How horrible to be responsible for people who perish in wars; but, to be responsible for the destruction of millions of souls for eternity is incomprehensible. Revelation 14:9-11. See Chapter on "Mark of the Beast."

Christians, once you read this book you can no longer say it is only a simple "Code Mark" put on products. "Marks" are already being manufactured in Cards, and Bar Codes are already being put on them. These will soon be upon all Cards to identify people; and, then what a small matter to transition the "Mark" on the Card to the person.

Secondly, PRAY for me! It is one thing to write about fulfillment of Bible Prophecy which deals with great and general concepts; the Middle East, end-time alignment of nations, perilous times; but, it is another to stalk constantly in the strong holds of Satan; identifying, and exposing the "nuts and bolts" used by the power houses of this world in their united effort TO CONTROL ALL THE MONEY! This is my posture. In the natural, I am totally awed contemplating the power of these great corporations. It is a replay; David and Goliath. Many times I have had to concur with the Apostle Paul in answering the somber call upon my life; *"None of these things move me, neither count I my life dear unto myself, so that I might finish my course with joy, and the ministry which I have received of the Lord Jesus ..." Acts 20:24.*

Thirdly, PRAY that all born again Christians will call for a Holy Convocation, blow the trumpet in Zion, proclaim a fast, call for a SOLEMN assembly and weep between the porch and the altar. PRAY that God will presently stay the hand of judgment, cause the sun to move backward, the moon to stand still, and preserve for our precious children yet a Godly heritage.

And finally, PRAY for our nation ... leading the world down the primrose path to the "Mark of the Beast."

FROM THE MOUNTAINS!
TO THE PRAIRIES!
TO THE OCEANS WHITE WITH FOAM!
GOD BLESS AMERICA!
OUR HOME SWEET HOME!

Notes

*Please send in any pertinent data which you feel is fulfillment of Bible Prophecy; especially as these relate to the economy, the dollar, Electronic Funds Transfer, the Card, the Mark, "666," (the Cashless System), etc.

*Christians who have questions regarding the use of Cards, statements, checks, or any vehicle or instrument incorporating the use of "666," please read the Chapter, "Six Hundred Three-Score and Six;" also, the Chapter, "The Mark of the Beast."

1 IBM's *Think Magazine*, April 1981.

• • • • •

THE "U.S.," SOCIAL SECURITY, IRS, and "666"

I have observed the "coy" usages of the Number "666" for years. For example, in 1977 the Internal Revenue Service Forms W-2P began requiring the prefix "666." Howls of protests from Christians arose. They deleted it in 1978 and 1979. In 1980, 1981, they slipped it back in. OOPS, Christians howled again! They said, "We didn't intend to offend anybody. We will delete it in 1982." It is an old game called, Wearing Resistance Down. And, while they may delete it in one place, it pops up all over. See pictures of a few of the U.S. Government's uses.

Department of the Treasury
Internal Revenue Service

1980

Instructions for
Forms W-2 and W-2P

Box 14.—IRA codes.—If box 9 is an IRA payment, enter **666.** Identify the kind of payment by showing one of the following code numbers after **666:** 1 for premature (other than disability or death); 2 for rollover; 3 for disability; 4 for death; 6 for other; 7 for normal; 8 for excess contributions plus earnings on such excess contributions; and 9 for transfer to an IRA for a spouse, incident to divorce. (For example, **6663** for disability.)

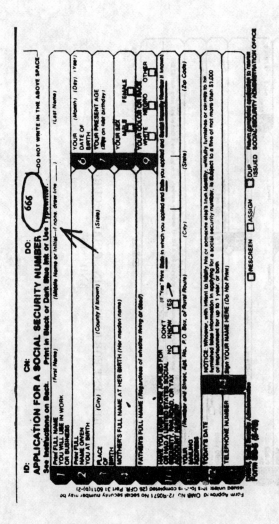

ID: APPLICATION FOR A SOCIAL SECURITY NUMBER. CR: DO: 666

See Instructions on Back. Print in Black or Dark Blue Ink or Use Typewriter.

DO NOT WRITE IN THE ABOVE SPACE

1 Print FULL NAME YOU WILL USE IN WORK OR BUSINESS
(First Name) (Middle Name or Initial—if more, draw line) (Last Name)

2 Print FULL NAME GIVEN YOU AT BIRTH

PLACE OF BIRTH (City) (County if known) (State)

YOUR DATE OF BIRTH (Month) (Day) (Year)

YOUR PRESENT AGE (Age on last birthday)

MOTHER'S FULL NAME AT HER BIRTH (Her maiden name)

YOUR SEX MALE FEMALE

FATHER'S FULL NAME (Regardless of whether living or dead)

YOUR COLOR OR RACE WHITE NEGRO OTHER

HAVE YOU EVER BEFORE APPLIED FOR A SOCIAL SECURITY NUMBER OR TAX ACCOUNT NUMBER? NO DON'T KNOW YES → (If "Yes" Print State in which you applied and Date and Social Security Number if known) (State)

YOUR MAILING ADDRESS (Number and Street, Apt. No., P.O. Box, or Rural Route) (City) (State) (Zip Code)

TODAY'S DATE

Sign YOUR NAME HERE (Do Not Print)

TELEPHONE NUMBER

NOTICE: Whoever, with intent to falsify his or someone else's true identity, willfully furnishes or causes to be furnished false information in applying for a social security number, is subject to a fine of not more than $1,000 or imprisonment for up to 1 year, or both

☐ RESCREEN ☐ ASSIGN ☐ DUP ISSUED Return completed application to nearest SOCIAL SECURITY ADMINISTRATION OFFICE

Form SS-5 (5-66)

Form Approved OMB No. 12-R0571 No social security number may be issued unless this form is completed (26 CFR Part 31 6011(b)-2)

SOCIAL SECURITY APPLICATION AND "666"

77

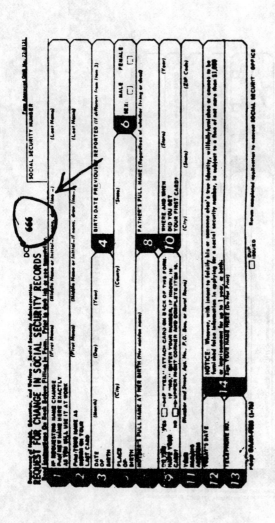

REQUEST FOR CHANGE IN SOCIAL SECURITY RECORDS
AND "666"

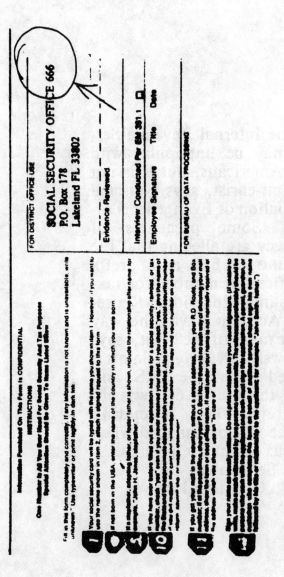

CONFIDENTIAL INSTRUCTIONS OF SOCIAL SECURITY
AND "666"

"The Internal Revenue Service may be unpopular with most Americans, but it is not the Anti-christ, says National Association of Evangelicals *Insight*. 'Some preachers of prophecy are alleging that the **IRS use of 666** as a prefix identification number for taxpayers in an Individual Retirement Account paves the way for the mark of the beast,' says the newsletter. *Insight* claims it checked with the IRS and found the use of 666 was inadvertent. The offending number will be changed when 1982 tax forms are printed."

September, 1981
Christian Life

"U.S. Treasury Department, Internal Revenue Service, Alcohol Tobacco and Firearms" Badge. The number "666" is at the bottom.

BEEP! BEEP! BEEP! BEEP!

"In one nanosecond (1/100,000,000 second) computing speed, . . . any bit of data from among billions of Numbers and Characters, may be almost instantly retrieved . . ." Britannica Encyclopedia 1981

There is an International Information Computer into which very difficult problems are entered; as, how to define the shadow of a teaspoon, or the transparency of a champagne glass with geometric equations, for the purpose of creating images in these likenesses. Discover Magazine, October 1980.

In Isaiah 8:19, the Prophet warned people against "seeking unto WIZARDS that PEEP and MUTTER" (computers) for advice, and not unto God. He grouped these with mediums.

CHAPTER II

THE MONEY CARD, THE MARK, AND "666"

"100,000 Words on a Strip, Card to Carry All Data"

"San Francisco (UPI) The narrow brown stripe on the plastic card that holds the SECRET KEY to your credit may soon carry all your other secrets as well.

Drexler Technology Corp., ... has developed a stripe, ONE-HALF INCH by THREE INCHES, that can carry five million bits of information or the equivalent of 100,000 words ... **Can you record a whole book on it? YES!**

Thus when you flash your card to pay a dinner bill or buy a pair of shoes, the readout might show those embarrassing overdrafts five years ago ... There are a number of applications ... the obvious ones are financial transactions of all types ... Additionally one could include your entire medical history, including a digital recording of electrocardiograms and all the medical records.

This quantum leap in card technology is well beyond

the development state. 'WE ARE NOW SELLING THE SYSTEMS,' said Mr. Drexler." *Daily News*, Van Nuys, CA, August 26, 1981.

Goodbye Credit Cards

"For what do the bells toll?" For the simple, convenient Credit Card, embossed on the front with only a name and a number. This Card is subtly, quietly being transitioned; first with the magnetic stripe, then with a Bar Code, into a Debit Card, which will eliminate all credit; an Identification Card which will include our life history; a Social Security Card, without which one can not be employed; and, a Money Card, without which one can not buy or sell. This combination WORLD WIDE MONEY CARD will become history's first successful effort to control mankind, with the built in capabilities to: monitor his every move; abolish all his privacy; refuse permission for gainful employment; and the key; to deny the privilege of "buying and selling."

"The technology is here!" After addressing a group in a University Town recently, an accounting major related to me: "In 1976, an official of the Federal Reserve Board conducted a seminar at Auburn University. All business, accounting, and computer technology students were invited. The course was entitled, The Cashless Society. The speaker was emphatic about the future of commerce being conducted in the total absence of cash. He indicated that the Fed's time table was five years to the implementation of this Cashless System. 'The technology is here,' he kept stressing, 'but the Sociologists have not yet prepared the people to be comfortable without money in their pockets.' "

This student indicated that he thought this Fed representative was way out in left field ... he indicated he has since changed his mind.

A renowned Computer Technologist confirmed to me in early 1980; "The Final Card is ready." What we are witnessing, however, seems to be a game of "Gradulism;" a gradual elimination of Cards (plural), Credit; and a tremendous acceleration in capabilities inherent in The Control Card.

We can expect to be told that The Money Card will micro-encode only information necessary to make intelligent financial decisions, on the mag stripe, and in the Bar Code; but, really, haven't astute decisions been made for a generation from just an embossed name and number run through a hand-powered impressionable machine?

Furthermore, who could write a book on just one's finances? I write an average of twelve checks a month; hardly a paragraph. So one immediately focuses on:

"WHAT WILL THEY WRITE ON MY ½″ × 3″ MAG STRIP BOOK? AND, WHO WILL BE ITS AUTHOR?"

The Mercy System

Christians grow accustomed to our Heavenly Father's knowing about those times when we falter and subsequently throw ourselves upon Him in repentance. We also abide in the comfort of knowing that He forgives us, blots out the sin, and remembers it against us no more. We trust this Author because He loves, forgives, deletes, and restores. His book on our lives is written with the pen of mercy.

But, how about the physician who must record the nervous breakdown, the attempted suicide, the abortion, and the like? The Medical Profession, for which I have great respect, is aware now that everything they write; symptoms, diagnoses, treatments, and prescriptions, are subject to open scrutiny, debate, and even litigation. Members of this profession will no longer be able to withhold information of which they will be cognizant can be personally demoralizing, if not damaging, once it is written. "To write or not to write" may be the name of many future games.

I remember times my late husband, a physician, would share with me that he felt he had been instrumental in preserving not only a man's dignity, but also his marriage, by not disclosing the diagnosis of veneral disease. He was indeed a "family" physician. These personal kindnesses will not be possible in the controlled System; so the physician, like the banker, like the government, of necessity must become brutally open; recording everything, releasing everything. What a demoralizing system. A single DWI will follow one a lifetime.

Somehow, in studying about this merciless System, my appreciation for our Heavenly Father's System grows. Oh, yes He forgives! Yes, He forgets! He even obliterates! and puts our sins in the Sea of Forgetfulness. Oh yes:

> "The Arm of my Savior is long,
> And the Love of my Savior is strong,
> And His GRACE so FREE, is sufficient for me,
> It's High as the mountain; It's Deep as the sea,
>
> ... And though millions have come,
> There's still room for One,
> Yes, there's room at the Cross for you!"

And before we examine this Control Card further, those of you who have never experienced the Long Arm of Christ removing the weight of your sins from you, and putting them into the Sea of Forgetfulness, come with me now to the Cross ... Central to Christ's System. The most descriptive words of my own personal experience were written by another:

> "At the Cross, At the Cross,
> Where I first saw the light,
> And the BURDEN of my heart rolled away,
> It was there by FAITH, I received my sight,
> And now I am happy all the day."

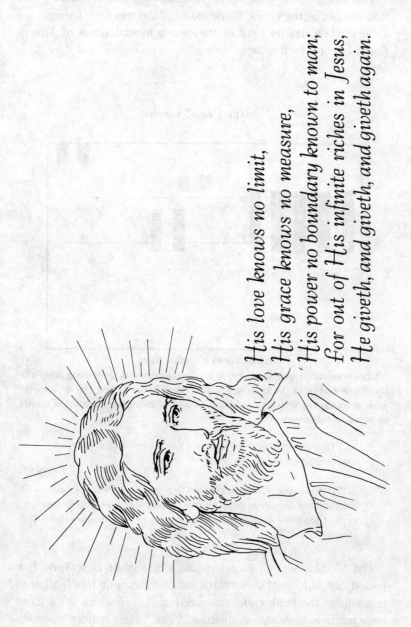

His love knows no limit,
His grace knows no measure,
His power no boundary known to man;
for out of His infinite riches in Jesus,
He giveth, and giveth, and giveth again.

This can be your experience; furthermore, that is where you'll find me yet, at the cross. Pause now ... and meet me there.

Meanwhile, let us look at the two principal types of Money Cards being issued today.

"Bar Code" Card

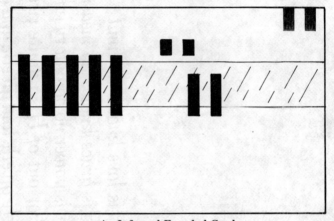

An Infrared Encoded Card
Under infrared photography, it looks transparent, revealing only the Bar Code put in at the time of manufacture. To the naked eye its appearance is opaque. (Artist's rendering of one of more than a million Cards encoded in this manner).

"To encode this Card; the core stock is printed with a 'Bar Code' that is different for every card."[1]

"The technique of making the card is secret. To do this, the bank built its own factories, using its own employees ... and complete control has been kept over the card, the reader, and the manufacturing process."[2]

The World's second largest bank, Citibank of New York, has issued one million of these cards nationwide using this "patented technology the bank calls 'the magic middle;'[3] which is "a fixed code put in at time of manufacture."[4] The "magic middle" consists of 55 rectangles encoded with information in a grid. The reader (an infrared beam) converts these into electronic pulses.

"666 Rodeo Day"
July 23, 1981, in Cheyenne, Wyoming.

In this infrared encoded card, the "Bar Code" in the card plus the information on the card (number, name, and date of issue), refer to a central file, all of which is used in making decisions.

Bar code symbol for cartons

"Bar Code" as shown in the *Pittsburgh Press,* June 21, 1981. This is pictured to illustrate only that the industry uses "Bar Code" for different types of encodations. This one is for identification of cartons in a warehouse setting.

This Card System has its advantages. It is a very difficult one to defraud. Citibank launched its efforts through its subsidiary, Transaction Technology, Inc., after a group of Cal Tech students easily defrauded the Mag Stripe Cards. Today, we have the "Magic Middle" versus the "Mag Stripe" Cards, two very different systems.

Citibank's Cards will not be accomodated by the banking industry's standardized magnetic stripe readers, and will not be helped any by the industry's requirement for all United States banks to be converted to mag tape by March, 1982. This banking organization, however, is a pioneer in new banking techniques as is evidenced by their advertisement in the Wall Street Journal, November 5, 1981, which reads:

> "A new banking era has begun. And Citibank invites you to be in the forefront ... A GLOBAL SYSTEM linking every major city in America to a bank with a financial service NETWORK THAT CIRCLES THE ENTIRE WORLD."
>
> Citibank
> GLOBAL ELECTRONIC BANKING

One of Citibank's officials commented on a one Super Card System thusly:

> "If there's just one card ...
> it will be issued by the government!"
> *Business Week*, April 18, 1977

The Mag Strip Card

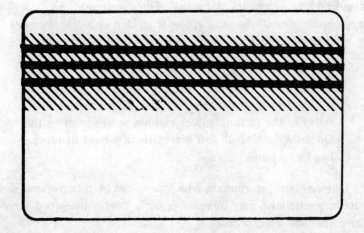

The 100,000 Word Book? Traditionally, it has carried three data tracks for encoding.

The magnetic strip Card is the standard bearer for the Card Industry, usually with from two to five data tracks where information is micro-encoded, *(secretized)*, and read by a machine. This type Card accounts for 33% of the 700 million Cards in use worldwide, and includes about every Card except the infrared encoded Cards.

In 1971, the American Bankers Association set standards for the magnetic strip encoding to be put on the backs of cards for the purpose of establishing a "National System" of Point of Sale credit. The "national" aspect soon gave way to an "international" intention.

On October 18, 1972, the *American Banker* published an article entitled, Magnetic Stripe Credit Card Encoding Nears World-Wide Test, in which it was announced that International Standards Organization had approved the ABA mag stripe criteria which would result in an international system of card usage.

"The magnetic stripe card is fundamentally a 'data carrier.'" *Spectrum*, 1974. We could say that this was the understatement of that decade. When each data track could carry only about one hundred bits, or twenty-five words. The acceleration in data storage capabilities of the mag stripe is rivaled only by advances in computers, of which a writer in the Washington Star said:

> "Had the automobile developed at a pace equivalent to that of the computer during the past 20 years, today a Rolls Royce would cost less than $3, get three million miles to the gallon, deliver enough power to drive the Queen Elizabeth II and six of them would fit on the head of a pin!"

Likewise, the information which now can be micro-encoded on the magnetic strip may increase from "a twenty-five-word secret" to a "100,000-word secret."

We see from Chapter I that every item manufactured will be identified by "Numbers" reduced to "Marks" in a Bar Code Symbol. Now, we see a person is identified by a Number plus a Bar Code made in the Infrared Encoded Card.

The big, big question has been all along, where will this "Bar Code" be incorporated on the banking industry's choice, the Magnetic Strip Card?

Certainly the information contained in the Bar Code could easily be micro-encoded in the mag stripe. But, my sources indicate that the Bar Code will be in **addition to** the mag stripe, VISIBLE to the unaided eye, and will require a separate device for scanning it. See picture.

Why? Far too many people; (employees of banks, card companies, and proprietary businesses) will have access to this "ho hum" financial-plus data. However, the Bar Code Symbol can contain secrets to which the bank clerks and the proprietors do not have access ... only those who control the System. Expect Bar Codes on Final Cards to be assigned by the Government, and the responsibility for issuing them given over to the Federal Reserve Banks.

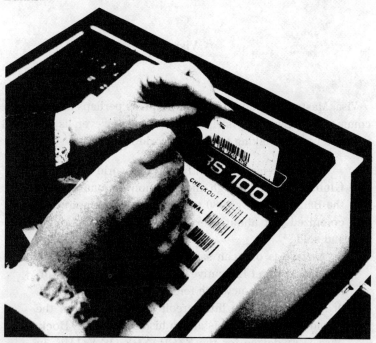

Magnetic Stripe—Bar Code Card

In the controlled environment of Baylor University, Waco, Texas, where a student can neither eat, read, swim, receive health care, or attend a football game without the All Purpose Card, with which to pay, gain access to the library, marina, health center or stadium, "a 'Separate Computer' reads the *Bar Code on the back of the Card, just above the magnetic strip,* makes a note of the student's number, and the titles of any books (also coded) that she is checking out." Bid Privacy Farewell, by Richard Coniff; *Next Magazine,* August 1981.

AUTHOR'S COMMENTS:

1. You can plainly see the Bar Code being scanned with a pencil-like reader. This Bar Code has to do with Life Style, (personal preferences); for example, the books one reads.
2. The magnetic tape (underneath Bar Code) must be read by another, the Central Computer. Its concern is primarily financial data, how promptly one pays his bills, etc.

Visa

Visa, MasterCard, and American Express perhaps are the most commonly known mag strip Cards. Visa, however, is the Card which is rapidly making the entire world its domain.

"A Visa executive recently said the world became 'a **Global** Village through the common denominator of the Bank Card.' By 1980 the far flung Visa empire had colonized just about everywhere things were bought and sold."[5]

"As fast as one can say Electronic Funds Transfer, Dee Hock, Chief Executive of Visa International, is off concocting some new use for the blue and white Card. 'It started out as a little credit card, which was the stupidest marketing mistake in history,' said Mr. Hock. 'Visa is a "device for the EXCHANGE OF VALUE. In short, **it's the next thing to money....**' His plan is to develop a PREMIUM CARD ... and to push expansion overseas. Comparing Visa with MasterCard and American Express, Mr. Hock's vision is considerably more cosmic: It's the first truly TRANS-NATIONAL CORPORATION. It's a WORLD-WIDE CONSUMER PAYMENT SYSTEM. What Mr. Hock has in mind is to link his member banks to consumers all over the world, who are willing, he said **'to pay a substantial price'** to be able to use a Card to exchange the VALUE OF ANY-THING ... FOR SOMETHING ELSE."

"From his office in San Francisco's TransAmerica Building earlier this year he cut up the world into three regional boards ... Each region's chairman holds a title appropriate to the culture Visa is infiltrating. Analysts said that in an effort to BURY THE COMPANY'S AMERICAN ORIGIN, Mr. Hock is even considering moving his office to London. Mr. Hock denied that ... Visa's new INTERNATIONAL CLOAK is crucial to its goal to saturate the GLOBE with its blue and white plastic."

Issuing Bank:
AUSTRALIA AND NEW

Your Bankcard Account Number:

J. P. Wright

496 01 234 567890

J P WRIGHT

VALID FROM 00 / 00   UNTIL END 00 / 00

↑ Card valid from the first day of the month shown

↑ Card expires on the last day of the month shown

"IN CASE OF LOSS: If your Bankcard is lost or stolen, immediately notify your Bank or, in New Zealand, any Bank displaying the BANK-CARD SYMBOL.

You can buy a wide range of goods and services wherever you see the colourful BANKCARD SIGN in Australia and New Zealand. You can obtain a cash advance during trading hours from any bank branch displaying the

BANKCARD SIGN, even if it isn't your bank. If travelling elsewhere, enquire about an overseas Bankcard.

CONDITIONS OF USE

. . . 5. A Bankcard will be honoured by banks and merchants displaying the SCHEME SIGN appropriate to the card produced."

The foregoing was taken verbatim off the literature accompanying an Australian Bank Card. The "Bankcard Symbol," "Bankcard Sign," and "Scheme Sign," are one and the same; a Logo configuration of "666."

THE SAME "666" configuration is on VISA in Australia.

Notice these things in particular:

1. Visa is "a device for the EXCHANGE OF VALUE;" a means of transacting business without using money; a substitute for money; a system which is conditioning the world to live without money.

2. "It's the next thing to money." (And, in the Electronic Funds Transfer System, it's as close as we shall ever get to money!!!)

3. "It's a World-wide Consumer Payment System." A system designed to transfer **Numbers** and **Value** amounts within a world-wide electronic communications network; a system of commerce whereby there would never be any shift made in the actual location of money.

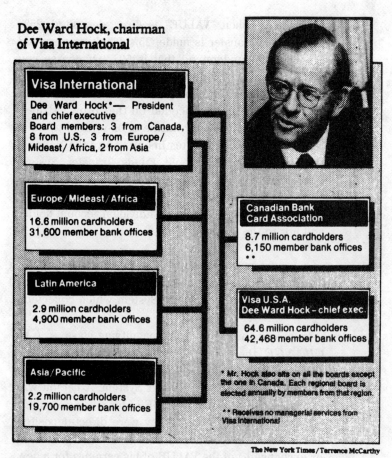

Dee Ward Hock, chairman of Visa International

Visa International
Dee Ward Hock * — President and chief executive
Board members: 3 from Canada, 8 from U.S., 3 from Europe/Mideast/ Africa, 2 from Asia

Europe/Mideast/Africa
16.6 million cardholders
31,600 member bank offices

Latin America
2.9 million cardholders
4,900 member bank offices

Asia/Pacific
2.2 million cardholders
19,700 member bank offices

Canadian Bank Card Association
8.7 million cardholders
6,150 member bank offices
**

Visa U.S.A.
Dee Ward Hock – chief exec.
64.6 million cardholders
42,468 member bank offices

* Mr. Hook also sits on all the boards except the one in Canada. Each regional board is elected annually by members from that region.

** Receives no managerial services from Visa International

The New York Times/Terrence McCarthy

New York Times, January 7, 1981, graphically depicts Mr. Dee Hock's Cosmic Vista for Visa International.

4. The user will pay:
   A. "**A substantial price** to be able to use a Card to exchange the VALUE of ANYTHING for SOMETHING ELSE."
   B. A substantial price? My sources have indicated that WHEN EFT if fully functional the user will pay a 25% fee for the VALUE he has exchanged for something else. One source calculated the fee to be a two-way

assessment; when "VALUE" is direct-deposited, 25%; and when a transfer is made, 25%. I believe a second grader could understand that is 50%. Of course you could never get this "officially" confirmed ... this is "their" business. You could never get all the personal data they have micro-encoded on the "brown stripe," about you which is your business, or we like to think it is. Dr. Alan Westin, in testimony before the National Commission on Electronic Funds Transfer System concurred:

"An individual's record should be valuable legal property belonging only to the individual account holder and not to the System."

However, in recent court cases, the decisions have been running to the contrary. Personal data do not belong to the individual about whom it is recorded, but to the System which collected it.

C.   Lets look at this one with a magnifying glass ... *EX-CHANGE* the *VALUE* of ANYTHING for SOMETHING ELSE. IN the final analysis EFT (the Cashless System) is a Worldwide Barter System. A person will exchange say 1/6 of the VALUE of his week's earnings which he never received; (they were direct-deposited to his ACCOUNT Number), for a basket of groceries; or exchange ⅓ of the VALUE of his earnings for a new coat. Now, neither merchant; the Grocer nor the Department Store Owner received any money ... only a debit value to their account Numbers (or Marks). History does repeat itself ... "Back In The Barter Again." You could sing that to the tune of ... Oh, well, remember there is humor to be found in everything, even EFT. "A merry heart doeth good like a medicine;" and with EFT? It will give headaches to aspirins.

Did you really get the picture? THE NEW MONEY SYSTEM?

"They have the money; we have the System. It's called Electronic Funds Transfer System. It is as though we are all children, dancing to their music, playing their game — and how!

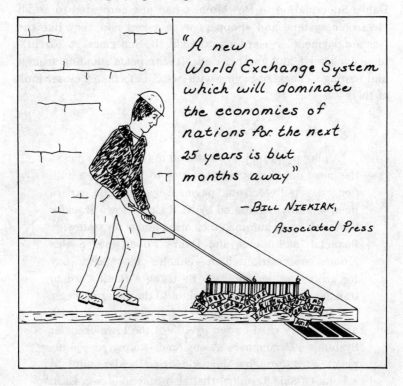

"A new World Exchange System which will dominate the economies of nations for the next 25 years is but months away"

— Bill Niekirk, Associated Press

Rave Reviews

People are rendering "rave reviews" at these consolidated services. Look for the Bank Windows when you go in one of the three Martins Food Stores in Washington County, Maryland. First Federal Savings and Loan Association of Hagerstown, MD is making "basic banking functions as easy as a trip to the supermarket." A Metroteller Card will transfer payment of groceries, but since the windows are manned, 85 hours of banking services a week are also provided. *Morning Herald,* Hagerstown, MD, September 30, 1981.

On Cable News Network, October 17, 1981, it was reported that Dahl's Supermarket in Des Moines, had just converted to an all electronic system, and shoppers were asked how they like the "instant payment" by Card instituted by the Supermarket. "Great!" once exclaimed; and another said; "It sure beats standing around and writing a check, or paying with cash." Let's take a closer look at this:

"A pilot program just kicked off in Des Moines marks the most ambitious attempt yet to establish a full-fledged, retail electronic-payment system. The experiment—jointly conducted by NCR Corp.; Iowa Transfer System Inc., an automated clearing house for statewide financial institutions; and Dahl's Foods Inc., a Des Moines supermarket chain—enables customers to pay for groceries electronically by using a Bank Card to transfer funds from their account to the supermarket's.

A Dahl's customer can pay his bill electronically with a proprietary card issued by 105 of the Iowa Transfer System's 592 members. A customer simply passes his plastic card through a Magnetic Stripe Reader built into a Point-Of-Sale Terminal that also functions as a Cash Register, punches in his personal identification number, and the amount of his tab is instantly transferred. More important, this is but the first of many significant efforts to automate retail transactions that are now in the works. Many financial and retail institutions are now predicting that electronic payment systems such as the one being tested in Iowa will become widespread during the 1980's. 'The payoff is there. It's just a question of how fast it develops,' says William J. Sinkula, Vice-President of finance at Kroger Co., the nation's second largest supermarket chain." *Business Week,* October 26, 1981.

When the Debit Card System ushers in full fledged EFT, the need for the PIN (Personal ID#) will be eliminated by the Number incorporated in the Bar Code. A combination Mag Tape Reader and Bar Code Scanner will give an instantaneous read-out for the dual coded Money Card.

The people in Iowa are a head's length in front of most states in EFT.

> "The Iowa Credit Union League has reached agreement in principle for its member credit unions to join Iowa Transfer System Inc. ... Shareholders of participating credit unions will be able to use the network of 122 electronic bank card terminals in BANKS, GROCERY AND OTHER RETAIL STORES to withdraw cash and make deposits in their accounts. Transfer System Director, Dale A. Dooley, said the technology is in place for a customer of an Iowa bank to make a cash withdrawal from an account in just about any part of the country. Dooley said he is confident the Iowa Transfer System will withstand the challenges of such large institutions as New York's Citicorp when interstate banking eventually is approved."

Never doubt that interstate banking will be approved, and soon! A letter in my file reads:

> "There was a full page advertisement in the *Detroit News* recently about 'Magic Money.' It is a new system of computer hook-ups by the Michigan National Bank. It permits other Bank Cards to be used in their 24 hour Automatic Bank Teller Machines outside of most banks. This points up that the 'hook-up' is almost finalized, and most of are conditioned to numbers and computers." David Kleefuss, *Grosse Pointe, MI November 2, 1981.*

If people would only look at the prognosis of EFT **when there is no alternative,** all would agree with my assessment; it is an insult to an intelligent society. I could conceive of suggesting such a System for a nation of illiterates, or people who are incapable of thinking and doing for themselves, but the scope of it should be limited to such applications.

Mastercard II

There are two primary money Cards which have saturated the world. The one enjoying the widest acceptance is Visa, with more than 90 million Card holders in the world; MasterCard is second. Both have worldwide networks, and may by a remote component interrogate the Central Information System and transfer data desired in a flash around the world. MasterCard may be second, but it is no slouch, as is indicated by their advertisements.

"MasterCard II, (a Debit Card), is accepted worldwide ... at close to 3,000,000 locations in more than 140 countries. MasterCard II works like a check. Only you never write the check."

EFT fully implemented will be operated by Debit Cards only!

"Within five to seven years, there will be more debit cards in America than credit cards," predicts Russell E. Hogg, President of MasterCard International, Inc. *Business Week*, October 26, 1981.

According to the Industry's top researchers, Frost and Sullivan, Inc., a more immediate phase out of Credit Cards can be expected. The Debit Card System effects a total elimination of all credit. It will be most like the check writing system, with no lag time for clearing checks. Instant withdrawal, but no writing of checks. In fact, the EFT System will not only be cashless, but paperless and proofless.

One of the most frightening aspects of EFT is that without paper, it will be difficult to prove anything. There will be no more cancelled checks, and the computer can be programmed to forget the payment; or by computer error have the memory of the transaction obliterated. Former Director of Communications for Bankamericard (now Visa) Mr. Terry Galanoy warns:

> "Protesting too loudly about it isn't going to help either, because that disturbance you kick up is going to end up in one of your files. And on that come-and-get-it day when we're all **totally and completely dependent upon our Card or whatever other survival device might replace it** ... You might be left all alone without one."[6]

American Express Card

I have for some time recommended that people apply for this Card for several reasons:

1. It is a Credit Card.
2. No limit is attached to purchases in a given period of time.
3. All purchases must be paid up monthly.

While we cannot know how long it will be before our purchasing power will be limited to One Card, there is some flexibility in this Card.

Visa and MasterCard Credit Cards have stated limits. With the precedent established, we can expect Debit Cards, (the Final Cards) to follow suit. It is already propounded that since all one's worth is vulnerable to one misuse, a daily limit will be established. In Montgomery, I have found withdrawal limits on Debit Cards to be from $25 to $200 per day. The amount is not as important as the principle. We are being condition to accept another's terms on how much money, of our money, we can withdraw at a given time.

When limits on Cards are imposed; and they will be, it could prove to be a great convenience, at least for a while, to hold onto the American Express. The hope is dim.

The Card Cartel

Of course, the time is approaching when all Card Systems will merge, use each other's equipment and issue Cards from a central office. The next **World Cartel to be formed will be the Card Industry.** Like the OPEC Cartel they will be answerable to the World Consortium. Why should VISA compete with MasterCard and invest millions on two separate systems? By joining they can share systems, and the division of profits will be greater for each because of reduction in equipment investments and personnel. **Competition** is becoming an ugly word, as is **Private Enterprise.** Sharing is Socialism. Sharing is "in." (Capitalism still feeds Socialism, however.)

Visa and MasterCard have been trying to get together for such a marriage. In 1979 the target date was set for 1982. The merger, like the Final Card, like the Cashless Society, could be delayed. Mr. Frank Lautenberg, Chief Executive Officer of Electronic Data Processing, Inc. was asked the question on Cable News Network, June 28, 1981, "What happened to the Checkless/Cashless Society that was supposed to have arrived by 1980?" He replied, "It was delayed ... Look for major changes in the mid 80's to bring about this paperless aspect ... Cable TV will greatly assist it."

First National Bank

WITHDRAWAL LIMIT

$25

Through week of October 31

In preparation for the Card Segment of EFT (Cashless Society) the banks have had all of the larger denominations of bills recalled. The Fed stopped printing large denominations ($500s, $1000s, $5000s, and $10,000s) after WW II. The Federal Reserve Board began recalling these in 1969. Today the largest denomination being printed is the $100 bill. Remember you did not read about this in the "approved media" releases. (No information amounts to "classified" information.) This point was brought home in 1980 when a man performed a service for us and required that we pay him in cash ... it amounted to several thousand dollars. (Have you tried to withdraw large funds from a bank recently? If you like adventure, you would enjoy it.) The cashier of the largest bank in Central Alabama informed us that they had nothing larger that day than $20 bills. I am going to leave the remainder to your imagination.

Actually the $100 bills are on the block now, thanks to Congressman Anthony Beilieson, (D.CA). If he has his way, we can say goodbye to them. He continues his effort toward the passage of his bill, HR. 2345, which would remove the $100 bills as legal tender. What subtle efforts people expend to usher in this Cashless Society! It appears every step toward detaching people from their money is a feather in some one's cap.

PATIENCE ZIGGY, PATIENCE

Need one say, the Government's interest in a Cashless Society can not be overstated. Uncle Sam is totally at the mercy of an individual when he transacts his business with cash. A person was recently convicted in Texas on income tax evasion because he operated a business with no checking account ... only cash receipts. The check writing system made the IRS jobs easy; the EFT System will put everything in their hands without the courtesy of the involved person being notified. **I give the illustration only to focus upon** the loss of Individual Control in the Cashless Society which is the commensurate gain of Government Control.

'QUICK COLLECTION. CUSTOMER OUT THERE WANTS TO CASH A TWENTY DOLLAR CHECK!'

Chip Vs. The Mag Strip

"But now a year before the **deadline is reached** for converting all **U.S. bank cards** to the magnetic tape, this technology is threatened with obsolescence. On the horizon are cards with integrated circuit chips imbedded in them for storage information so that the card can be updated each time it is used," states *Business Week*, February 23, 1981.

The major deterrent here is costs. This Chip Card would cost $20 to $60, while the mag strip card costs about 60¢. Also, banking and business industries have geared up with electronic readers to accomodate the mag stripe at great costs, which would have to be written off if the Chip Card were to replace the mag stripe at this juncture. Since Cards (as we now know them) are projected to be around only about three more years, (see topic, "The Demise of The Card") expect these two primary types, the Infrared Encoded, and the Mag Tape Cards, to dominate the industry.

The Money Card

Although great variations exist in "the manufacturing process of these two types of Cards, the end results of encodings and Bar Codes, when read by appropriate equipment, appear to the naked eye as unidentifiable "Marks." But in these will be your data; your identification.

With little or no resistance from the consumers, the UPC Marking System became so widespread, that from the date the Symbol was selected April 3, 1973, to 1977, 90% of grocery items, and many other manufactured products bore the UPC "Marks." Now, this

"Marking" phenomenon has spread its tenacles into the Card Industry, the means by which we shall pay for these "Marked" goods.

The Picture Worth 10,000 Words!

Part of an advertisement by National Cash Register run in Business Magazines in April, 1980. This very fine company writes much in this ad about their leadership in Financial Terminals. What they do not say however, is worth 10,000 words. It is prophetic. The picture depicts the different monies of the world being replaced by a simple piece of plastic. NCR calls it the WORLD WIDE MONEY CARD. Right on, NCR, right on!

There does remain a major problem with the Mag Stripe Card, fraud. Fraud in the mechanics of the System makes it vulnerable to false ID's, computer thefts and wiretapping devices. Because of the ease with which false ID's may be obtained, there will soon be the requirement to link people personally to their Card.

Linking People to Plastic

Traditional Identification Systems are grossly inadequate to deal with this modern, fast paced, amoral society in which no absolutes exist; no rights, no wrongs; nothing is holy, nothing profane. Everything is relative. Yes means maybe, and no conscience is pricked. Even marriage vows are made with escape clauses. "The heart is deceitful above all things, and desperately wicked."

Admittedly, we live in a perverted society. (Christians know that our citizenship is not of this world.) This society, for example, demands Government subsidies be given to the poor, but from the ranks of those same compassionate ones are a few who bilk large portions of that designed for the needy through fraudulent identification. Worse yet, the problem is growing.

It has been estimated that for each $5.00 appropriated for foodstamps, $1.00 reaches those for whom it was intended. The Foodstamp Program ballooned from half a million recipients in 1965 receiving $36 million to 20 million in 1976 receiving $6 billion. Between 1973-1975, Massachusetts did not investigate one case for fraud. Although, a Federal Audit revealed 50% of the recipients were ineligible and obtained checks with false ID's.

One year in New York, in excess of 1 million went to people receiving welfare checks obtained by fraud or foodstamps illegally. This was cut to $100,000 by requiring recipients to have photo ID cards, which now is beginning to be required nationwide.

Also, people move to new areas and leave all debts and child support to be absorbed by those left behind. With one all purpose

110

Card which identifies the person, this will be eliminated. An 800-page report by a Federal Advisory Committee on False Identification indicates false ID's are easy to obtain. In it we learn that many obtain multiple driver licenses. To the young, this seems to be a status symbol; with one license dated back a few years to gain alcohol and porno privileges, and to spread out driver infractions on more than one license. Criminals obtain aliases easily with which they can do banking and check cashing by several names. Some do this to cheat on income taxes.

There is of necessity a great drive on the part of the Government to crack down on both types of offenders. But, when the rich cheating on taxes, and the poor cheating on welfare, read about Congressmen involved in ABSCAM, they reason the pot should not call the kettle black. Yet, two wrongs never make a right. It is still *"righteousness which exalts a nation. Sin is still a reproach to any people." Proverbs 14:34.*

Oh, that we could learn everytime a dishonest act is committed, our society suffers. This is why offenders were severely punished or eliminated in Old Testament Israel. God knew only one immoral person could contiminate the whole of society. Today each act of dishonesty from shoplifting to embezzling forges us one step nearer the frightening aspects of the totally controlled society foretold by the Prophet John who saw that:

> *"Power (control) was given him (the World Dictator) over all kindreds, and tongues, and nations." Revelation 13:7*

All of the abuses by individuals are playing into the hands of the International Consortium which is promoting this New World Economic Order facilitated by the Society for Worldwide Interbank Financial Transactions (SWIFT), the EFT network.

But, so long as Federal handouts are necessary for votes; so long as business people cheat on income taxes, so long as there is a major criminal element in this country, there will be fraud; and with the advantages of the computerized society at the Government's disposal, this fraud will be dealt with in short order by

the Money Card with Pesonal Identification. The questions now
are not if a person will be linked to plastic, only when and how.

Smile, You're on "Control" Camera

The issuance of a World Wide (ID) Card has been delayed, as
has been the projected inception of a totally Cashless Society,
while officials search frantically for an acceptable, economical,
fast and easy Personal Identification device to be used in conjunction with this Card. (The Card, without personal ID, was ready
in early 1980, and the network to facilitate its use was intact.)

The first step in linking an individual to plastic will be via photography; the second step will entail body characteristics; and like
it or not, the proof of our identity in the near future will rest with
computers.

Forty-four states now have a photo drivers license program,
and some states issue non-drivers license for ID purposes to handicapped and senior citizens. The *New York Times* reported in their
October 9, 1981 edition, that:

> **"Photo ID Card to be required for food stamps.**
> **New York City estimates that** 2,500 authorization
> Cards a month are stolen and that use of photo Iden-
> tification Cards should eliminate most of these illegal
> transactions. States that require photographs on driver's
> license or on Identification Cards used in the public
> assistance program may adapt these documents for the
> food stamp program. More than 1.1 million residents
> of New York City get food stamps."

The *New York Times*, November 1, 1981, indicated a "Bank Card
for Food Stamps" would be issued to 13,000 welfare recipients to
introduce them to "the magic of electronically transferred funds."
The Card will have a "photograph, invisible signature, and a micro

encoded Number." Four branches of Manufacturers Hanover Trust Bank are participating in the experiment. "If proven successful, the new System could link banks, city agencies and welfare beneficiaries in a single Electronic Network. Furthermore, the new security features could set the NATIONAL STANDARD FOR WELFARE DISBURSEMENT." (I have been telling people for years to get out of debt and live within their means. The poor, the prisoners, the military, and possibly the Social Security recipients will be the initial guinea pig segments of society when EFT is begun to be enforced.)

Our first conditioning in Personal Identification is well underway with instant photography available. DEK/ELECTRO photographic ID programs are installed in eleven nations, and are under study in several others. This fine Corporation states that it is currently:

> "Testing several systems directed to a commercial, World-Wide mass market ... NOT DIRECTLY RELATED TO THE MANUFACTURE OF PHOTO CARDS; the advance technology required in the evolution of these new products was derived from the company's involvement in photo ID Cards."

We shall subsequently discuss Worldwide Mass Market ID beyond the photographic step. Meanwhile, the Photo ID now has the advantages of requiring no further equipment purchases for the business, and little training on the part of the employee reading the Card. The latter will also prove to be a disadvantage; little training, little accuracy; especially in view of counterfeit driver's license, and all kinds of other ID devices being sold at cheap shops all over the United States assisting the underground false ID network. It will ultimately require Computer Identification of facial features; and in addition, the next step, signature dynamics, fingerprinting, or hand scanning to be used in conjunction with the Money (ID) Card.

"The nation's most advanced INSTANT ID camera"

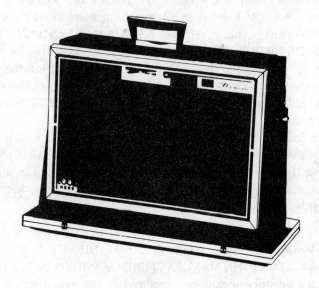

Finger Please!

Mastercharge conducted a study in San Francisco in 1973 to determine if people would respond negatively to their Credit Card if its use accompanied a required fingerprint. They did; since which time much money has been spent and energy expended to produce another acceptable form of ID for the Card.

Signature dynamics has proven one thing; there are too many people with expertise in forging others' names to rely solely on a signature for identification; although signatures will be required on The Money-ID-Cards. These will be verified by computers whose accuracy rate has reached 80%, but it will be almost incidental to identification. Speech analysis has also been disappointing in Personal Identification. Voices change with age, colds, diseases and surgery.

Graphicists are Computer Artists who feed numerical data into computers which translate these into images. All anatomical features of the body can be "defined" by algebraic and geometric formulas with which computers can render almost exact images. The image of President Lincoln here is "spatially quantized."

Computer identification of mass population may be done by much simpler techniques; as a nose can be judged on a scale of 1-10, the longest being 10. With several areas of facial features identified by numbers, the numerical data fed into a computer can verify the identity of a photograph. Once facial features are defined by numbers, computers have the capability of doing a "composite" of a person.

Unfortunately you can't identify a person with anything he has or knows; as a card, key, password or Personal Identification Number, PIN. Even though a Card may have a hundred thousand words about a person, it can not identify him. The Mag Strip can even be removed, and placed on another's Card without being discovered by the System. All the auxiliary items designed to assist in ID may also be lost, forgotten, stolen, or forged.

Only by a physical application of a finger print or hand scan, defined by computer bits (language); encoded on the Card, and verified at the time of a purchase, can this escalating fraud be reduced to a drizzle. Fingerprints do not change with age or physical condition. There are no duplicates!

A few minor problems play havoc with computer verification of finger printing as: gaining or losing weight, which adds or deletes lines; and arthritic, paralyzed, or deformed hands; and, armless persons. However, there still remains one giant obstacle to fingerprinting; the long standing stigma due to its association with law violators. Fingerprints-prisoners, are almost thought of simultaneously. Just as Mastercharge discovered in 1973, I predict people will continue to respond negatively, and resist mass fingerprinting per se of the public. An interesting observation is made by Mr. George H. Warfel:

> "If any of these (methods of fingerprinting) could be made to appear that the Identifyee was only pressing an 'action' button and not presenting the finger for examination, the public might be fooled into ready acceptance ... To achieve this, contact will have to be reduced to a fraction of a second, and position must not be critical. Perhaps such a device is being designed."[7]

Finger Scan Machine

With third down and one to go the team will try again to produce a Card with a convenient, acceptable identifying device. They will make a first down with the untainted, but successfully tested, finger/hand scan machines. "They're neat," I can hear the world saying ... "finally a machine that will keep them honest."

> "When a subject puts his finger on the glass plate of a Fingermatrix machine, an image of the print appears on a silver mirror and is scanned by a laser. A computer picks out about 40 tiny spots on the print, known in the trade as minutlae, and compares them with records stored in its memory."[8]

This article in *Wall Street Journal*, May 21, 1981, indicates further that this company:

> "... May have leaped ahead of International Business Machines, Texas Instruments Inc., and some other big corporations working on what are called biometric access controls. The category includes systems to identify people through such other traits as voice, hand geometry or handwriting."

Notice these are called "biometric access" systems. This sounds so upstanding and professional. "Bio" is a Greek prefix meaning "life." These systems will insure that the person is living, and is who he purports to be. Fingermatrix has one system operating at Chase Manhattan Bank presently.

We cannot undersell this technique! The application of Finger Scan is being considered as a means of Identification for worldwide **financial** and **access control.** One reputable private company whose officers invented much of the security technology for our Government, emphasizes in writing that their Finger Scan System can:

> "PROTECT A BUSINESS, PROTECT A BUILDING, ... you can even protect an **ENTIRE COUNTRY** from the entry of unauthorized persons ... And a SINGLE programmed computer station, located ANYWHERE in the world, can control as many remote terminals as you need."[9]

With this almost instant, clean technique, Finger Scan has much going for it. But, one can lose a finger, and since working in the yard over a weekend will so mar and tear the lines in the finger, machine verifications can be delayed for three to four days, I propose those who control the Electronic Fund Transfer System will opt for the Hand Scan Machine.

Hand Scan Machine
One of the models presently in use. The readout verifies one's individual hand geometry with a master file where measurements have been pre-determined, and reduced to code via a Bar Code or Mag Tape.

Hand Scan Machine

It does not take the student of Bible Prophecy long to assess that with the lateness of the hour, and the accelerating developments toward a Cashless System, of necessity we must be near the time when the masses will begin being conditioned to the surrender of their right hand in the Identification process for making financial transactions. Dr. Ray Brubaker, in his book, "Is the Antichrist Now Here?" confirms this:

> "In Cincinnati, Ohio, an experiment was conducted in which there was affixed on the back of each hand a number that was read by a scanner in the super market where these people did their shopping. As each item was checked out, the cash register simultaneously flashed it to the proper bank, where it was automatically deducted from that person's account."[10]

The $975 Report

It has been about as difficult to obtain documented information about the origin and development of the Hand Scan Machine as about the Universal Product Code. Of course, I respect trade secrets in a competitive environment. When all other research failed to turn up "desired data," an announcement of:

> **"An in-depth report analyzing and forecasting the: Access Control and Personal Identification (PI) Products Market in the U.S."** (In the report it was announced that) "Some approaches are already in use and others **are being tested and scheduled for implementation during the 1981 to 1984 time frame.** ... Some 75 companies involved in the market are identified in the report ... What means of access con-

trol and personal ID are planned in the future; (and) THE NUMBER OF HAND GEOMETRY SYSTEMS SOLD. 153 page report, Summer 1981, ... $975.00."

The price? Well, we opted to pay it without hesitation to establish for Christianity once and for all that the technology is here.

This report came enclosed in a simple spiral bound notebook. It was obviously compiled by a very elite group of researchers which had no sinister motives. It is intended for serious study by corporate/industrial organizations which can profit by its disclosures in spite of the $975 price tag.

In the report is written that there is:

> "... One system ... using hand geometry. The method was invented in 1972 and marketed by the inventor. **The System is perfected,** has withstood the tests of time in school cafeterias, where it was used in conjunction with meal cards with good success ... it is being vigorously marketed ... there are only **300 units presently in use.**"[11]

A man visited our office recently and told us of observing the hand scan machine in operation at the University of Georgia Cafeteria. He indicated that the meal cost was electronically transferred from the account of the student to the cafeteria's at the time the student's hand was verified in the machine ... providing adequate funds were available.

Beyond the Hand Scan

This Report further indicates that many giant corporations including Honeywell, Johnson Controls, Baker Industries, Burns and Wackenhut are already **LOOKING BEYOND THE CARD SYS-**

TEM into **"Personal Identifications Systems using OTHER THAN CARDS!"**

> "Wackenhut has acquired a hand geometry system, and Baker has a signature dynamics system for entry ID. These two companies will have the protection of operating experience with Personal Identification methods, when CARDS START TO YIELD TO AUTOMATED ID."[12]

What shall we say then? Portent of things which must shortly come to pass! I suggest you read this section several times! It will begin to penetrate ... what the giants of the industry are saying!

The author has chosen to omit naming the fine organization which markets the hand scan machines and the names of many other institutions which we have in our files using them. It is not these organizations which are evil, any more than one's participation in Social Security is evil; it is a World Wide Satanic Conspiracy (begun in the Garden of Eden when Eve was deceived) that is culminating in the alignment of all commerce today toward accomodating Satan's plan. The cunning thrust is that Satan has desired to be worshipped since he rebelled against God saying:

> *"I will exalt my throne above the stars of God; I will be like the most High!" Isaiah 14:13-14.*

Satan has deceived business people, professionals, bankers, scientists and technicians into implementing his age-old plan. He will ultimately succeed in gaining the WORSHIP of the world through the Electronic Funds Transfer System the industries of the world are developing. The Apostle John marveled that:

> *"**ALL** that dwell upon the earth shall worship him, (this last Super World Dictator), whose names are not written in the book of life ..." Revelation 13:8*

This universal worship of Satan will be short lived ... it will consummate in the Battle of Armageddon, (See charts in back of book.) He will be bound for a thousand years during which time his principal activity "deception" is abolished, but notice that ALL OTHER SINS CEASE! Revelation 20:3 & 8. All other sins (greed, murder, rape, robbery, forgery, etc.) are therefore the result of first being deceived.

> *"Let no man deceive you by any means . . ." II Thessalonians 2:3.*

The Demise of the Cards

In Frost and Sullivan's $975 Report, the Card System as we know it, is assessed to be on its last legs. Commenting on a good, economical method of Personal Identification to REPLACE or AUGMENT the present Plastic Card System, the report states:

> "IF SUCH A DEVICE IS TEN YEARS AWAY, **THE CARDS WOULD CONTINUE PAST** 1985; . . . If a good ID device should hit the market in 1982, **THE PLASTIC CARD MARKET** would have to join with the **NEW METHOD** to continue growing. The market (for Plastic Cards) is expected to continue at a real growth of 30% per year **AT LEAST FOR THREE YEARS.**"

And there we have it. Ladies and Gentlemen; the most astute researchers who sell their forecasts to the industries able to profit from buying such assessments, indicating the "handwriting" is on the wall for the Credit Card Industry . . . "weighed in the balances and found wanting."

Whatever the "good ID device" is, which could hit the market in 1982, we can be sure it will bring us one step closer to "defining and requiring" the perfect ID system, the "Mark" on the body.

Electronic Fund Transfer is Inevitable

The Electronic Fund Transfer System (Cashless Society) is inevitable, with all its accompanying ramifications. Not because it is the means by which a few will gain control over all the money in the world via International Electronic Networks, but because the prophecies of the Bible foretold it to be the means by which commerce would be conducted in the last Economic System of the present Age — just prior to Christ's return to the earth.

This EFT System, to be oerpated first with a Debit Card, will be borne out of supposed great necessity. John J. Reynolds, President of Interbank Card (MasterCard) Association said in April, 1979:

> "We have to begin to reduce the amount of paper that is passing back and forth. Total EFT is really just around some future corner."

> "The volume of transactions has become so enormous that transfer by means of an electronic pulse at the rate of thousands of bits per second is the new necessity, the new system for the worldwide EXCHANGE of VALUE," Philip Hayman, a Visa official, added.

Toward this end, bankers, card companies, computer technicians, and electronic engineers have pooled their efforts to produce One Card and One Code which will transcend differences in transmission, and reader systems. I expect the World Card to be a Magnetic Strip Card with a Bar Code, if only for the sake of economy. Since the System, at some future point, will be seized by Satan's Man of Sin, I expect a Bar Code facsimile to incorporate an identifying Mark of this Man's Name. (See Revelation 14:11). The Mark could be a Luciferean Star. The Number of his name will also be used. It will not take wisdom to identify his "Mark," but, to count the Number, "666," which obviously will be "veiled" from open view.

Of this you can be sure; you need look no further, the Electronic Funds Transfer System will be the "666 System." Now it will require wisdom and knowledge to be able to discern this end-time deceit. Don't look for it to be flaunted openly. Neither think that the simple will ever see, understand or believe it ... *"None of the wicked shall understand, but the wise (righteous) shall." Daniel 12:10.* Remember John said, one would need wisdom and understanding to *"Count" this usage of "666,"* which would be the clue. *Revelation 13:18.* Of ministers and teachers who continue to pass this Number "666" off as a mere computer coincidence or superstition; shun them! The *"strong delusion"* has deceived them, *II Thessalonians 2:11.* For those who declare you will know nothing about this as the Church will be "raptured out of it," pray for them ... THIS IS EXACTLY WHAT THE DEVIL WANTS THEM TO PREACH. PRAY THAT GOD WILL REMOVE THE BLINDERS FROM THEIR EYES.

SWIFT

Institutions are shadows of men. The EFT System is the shadow of a few people; international bankers, business people, and scientists, who have planned to appear to be able to solve the world's problems with the elimination of cash. Most people who will be sold on the System will never stop to think that WHEN WE ARE DETACHED FROM OUR MONEY, IT WILL BE SO THAT THEY CAN ATTACH THEMSELVES TO IT. Where will the real money go during this time? One guess. That's The New Money System.

The kingpins of banking are agreed that the international EFT network will be augmented by the Society for Worldwide Interbank Financial Transactions (SWIFT). A vast banking network with NO VAULTS, NO CASH. It is a System for large transfers. ... interbank activity. "VALUE EXCHANGES" will be ordered by these bank (?) computers, and numbers will be juggled when transactions are consummated. Ghost Banks. (Not enough in one

to attract the robbers.) *"Clouds they are without water." Jude 12.*
But, this is what the bankers have conjured up for us in order that
they might finally at last get their heart's desire ... All the money
of the world.

Since SWIFT is to UNIVERSAL ELECTRONIC BANKING what
the Bar Code is to UNIVERSAL ELECTRONIC SHOPPING, let us
look at some details of this Worldwide Banking Network.

Carl Reuterskiold, General Manger

**SWIFT MANAGEMENT COMMITTEE (L. to R.)—Enic O'Brien, Bessel
Kok, Carl Reuterskiold, Jacques Cerveau, and Jack Tilley.**

"The S.W.I.F.T. organization is the culmination of a range of studies initiated in 1969 with the aim of providing an improved international *payments system* ...

In May 1973, some 240 of the largest European and North American banks set up the Society for Worldwide Interbank Financial Telecommunication (S.W.I.F.T.) with the aim to design, implement and operate an *international financial network*. This enables member banks to transmit between themselves international payments, statements and other messages associated with international banking." Carl Reuterskiold, October 19, 1977.

"S.W.I.F.T. is a *co-operative society* created under Belgian law and registered in Brussels. It is *wholly owned by the member banks*, the shares being distributed at present according to anticipated traffic and ultimately according to actual traffic transmitted via the network ... There is a team based in Brussels who prepare instruction material and visit countries to assist National User Groups with educational courses, seminars and workshops.

Each S.W.I.F.T. country has its own internal organization which differs according to national requirements. Most countries have national member and user groups who meet regularly to review current progress. Each country has at least one User Group Representative who is nominated by the users and is usually an employee of a member bank or *national banking association*. He is the focal point for S.W.I.F.T. liaison. "S.W.I.F.T., F20 160 Second Edition, January, 1977.

NEWS RELEASE

BRUSSELS, Belgium, October 19, 1977—Lawrence A. Goshorn, President and Chairman of General Automation, Inc., headquartered in Anaheim, California, today represented the company at the official dedication for the large *international funds transfer network owned and operated* by **S.W.I.F.T., the Society for Worldwide Interbank Financial Telecommunications.**

"Today's opening ceremony marks the creation of a common international banking language," indicated Goshorn ...

"We become involved with S.W.I.F.T. at inception of the project, and were **one of the vendors selected to provide computer-based systems that allowed member banks to connect into the network and communicate with each other,**"said Goshorn.

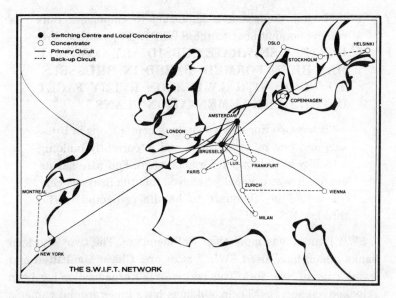

THE S.W.I.F.T. NETWORK

- ● Switching Centre and Local Concentrator
- ○ Concentrator
- —— Primary Circuit
- ---- Back-up Circuit

"The Network, in its first phase, covers most of Western Europe and North America. It is a two-centre financial *transaction control system,* the banks connecting their terminals to programmable concentrators in each country . . . Although each operating centre features fully duplicated computer configurations, a two-centre design is used for increased security should one centre become unavailable through natural catastrophe, industrial action or sabotage, each configuration has enough capacity to handle the entire traffic load." S.W.I.F.T., F20 160, January, 1977.

General Automation provided the interface devices enabling the System to "communicate by magnetic tape with other computers to exchange data . . ."

Burroughs Corporation wrote in *Future Developments of SWIFT, 1977:*

"The S.W.I.F.T. network cutover has now taken place, live messages are being transmitted, and, with S.W.I.F.T., Burroughs are looking forward to the time when all current Member Banks will be connected to the system, and beyond that to the inclusion of other banks and other countries, **until the system becomes truly *world-wide.***

127

"In this context it is important to emphasize Burroughs commitment to the S.W.I.F.T. project. **A COMPLETELY SEPARATE SUBSIDIARY COMPANY HAS BEEN FORMED, BASED IN BRUSSELS, TO WORK WITH S.W.I.F.T. ON EVERY FACET OF THEIR IMPLEMENTATION PLANS.**"

"It has two European switching centers, one in Brussels and one in Amsterdam, and is currently building a facility in Culpepper, Virginia where Fed-wire has its center. It was originally believed that the Brussels center would be adequate to handle projected traffic through 1985 . . ."[13]

SWIFT today has more than 700 members. The two American banks which have used SWIFT most are: Chase Manhatten and Irving Trust of New York. This entire SWIFT organization has been "cloaked" in secrecy. Their buildings have underground cameras all around them, closed circuit TV monitors, sensor devices which go off if a person starts running, and underground facilities with battery capacity sufficient to operate the entire network. (Over $70 billion daily is transferred through the Culpepper, Virginia Center already, the third Switching Center in the "Beast" Network.) This System uses "Packet Switching" which enables the Networks to communicate using different types of equipment, which represents "a true 'STATE OF ART' development in the field of international banking," said H. Hasselblad, Chairman of SWIFT.

"In early 1982 we are ready to believe every country in the world will be connected in one way or another to SWIFT," Dr. T. Hugh Moreton says in SWIFT: BANKING AND BUSINESS.

No doubt this accounts for the gloomy outlook in decentralized banking circles.

"The 1400 commerical banks that exist today will dwindle to fewer than 100 important institutions ... by the 1990's," states banking analyst, Thomas Thamara.

Nevertheless, SWIFT is for sure tailor made for EFT, since EFT IS A NO-CASH SYSTEM FOR THE MASSES; BUT, AN ALL-CASH SYSTEM FOR THE DESIGNERS ... THOSE FEW WHO CONTROL EFT AND US; and, the group which is now embarking on a program to sell EFT to the public.

Some Say No!

So many millions of dollars have been spent already on EFT that if not sold to, it would be forced upon us. But, EFT will require great finese to sell:

"Lack of a clear incentive to consumers has been a problem in the past and getting them to shift to electronic payment will probably require new pricing strategies and extensive advertising campaigns."[14]

Cornell Law School Professors Norman Penney and Donald Baker said of EFT:

"There has been something less than enthusiastic customer acceptance of some of the services offered."[15]

Time and again it has been brought to the attention of the Industry that people do not want it! For example, the state of Texas in a referendum, turned down EFT by a 2 to 1 vote. Some large banks and Saving & Loans in the West, and Mid-West found customer acceptance so light that they dropped their test programs a few years back. But, the System continued to promote EFT, until presently so much has been spent to facilitate it that the drive is now on to shift people's attention away from the slavery of the System to some overt, apparent advantages. Expect banks to begin to exploit the conveniences with full page ads about "instant money 24 hours a day!" Additionally, other subtle incentives like

129

check-cashing privileges will become expensive. Already in Syracuse, New York, people have been penalized up to $3.00 per transaction for making payment by check or cash as opposed to EFT. The Federal Reserve Board got into the act on August 1, 1981, when it decided to begin charging everyone more for clearing paper transactions (checks) than for automatic clearing house services, "because it wants to encourage the use of electronic payments systems." *Business Week*, August 3, 1981. Note this on your bank statements. In New York the cost will run between ½ and 5¢ per check.

When you have had time to count the COST of cash, and CHECK WRITING versus EFT, expect an overture of say 1% discount on all purchases made via EFT. The sad thing is some people will buy it and praise the convenience of "direct deposit," etc. . . . And once the public gets in it, there will be no retreating. The lion will close his mouth.

Expect the most stupendous EFT sales jobs to come from:

1) THE GOVERNMENT. Already the Social Security Department is doing a series of TV ads showing little elderly ladies picking up their Social Security Check from the mail box and being met by a "grizzly thug" demanding it. Then they add that Direct Deposit is so simple, safe and efficient.
2) THE BANKING INDUSTRY.
3) THE CREDIT CARD COMPANIES.
4) SOCIOLOGISTS. Let us look at an article from the *Los Angeles Herald Examiner*, April 28, 1981, written **by Leon M. Ledsman, entitled:**

"Here's An (Almost) Foolproof Cure for Crime:
Eliminate Cash"

"We are witnessing a barrage of News-media concern and debate about violent crime and its effect on the

ELECTRONIC BANKING
Networks for retail banking
Making money from transactions
Page 70

Here it comes!!! The NATIONAL BANK CARD
Business Week, January 18, 1982, on its cover, depicts A SINGLE CARD (debit card) for nationwide electronic banking. Quoting from the article: "One month ago key executives from a dozen of the largest U.S. and Canadian banks flew to a *secret* meeting at Chicago's O'Hare Hilton Hotel to form a joint venture that would create the first National Retail-Banking Network . . . The new networks should be far more powerful than Visa and MasterCard because they will operate with the debit card."

quality of life in the United States ... Yet there is a simple solution that would INSTANTLY result in a drastic reduction in crime ... THE SOLUTION IS TO ELIMINATE CASH ... Consider this: At a predetermined time, all cash would have to be surrendered to banks, acting as agents of the Treasury. Every citizen would be assigned a THIEF-PROOF ACCOUNT CARD ... The credit would be registered in central computers. All future transactions ... newspapers, subway fares, investment, new cars, dinner out — would be recorded much as they are now with Credit Cards, EXCEPT THAT THE TRANSACTION WOULD INSTANTLY debit the purchaser and credit the seller. (Debit Card) Every business, store, street corner, could have a TRANSACTION BOX ... Bank robbery vanishes. Embezzling gets harder. The disappearance of cash would complicate ... the vast multi-billion-dollar trade in illegal drugs. ... There are many problems ... Computer fraud, already a serious problem, would result in continuous contests between bad guys and the protectors of the System.

... The penalites have traditionally been the erosion of PRIVACY and FREEDOM OF ACTION.

... This proposal is another step in the direction of being asked to place even MORE TRUST IN THE GOVERNMENT."

Pictured along with this article was a Card entitled: MONEY.

The "Irreversible" Card

The Debit Card with Personal ID will be the Card by which buying and selling will be conducted when EFT is fully opera-

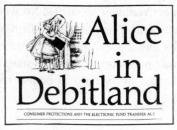

Alice
in
Debitland

CONSUMER PROTECTIONS AND THE ELECTRONIC FUND TRANSFER ACT

The **BOARD OF GOVERNORS** of the Federal Reserve System, June, 1980, printed a booklet entitled *Alice in Debitland*, explaining and encouraging the use of Debit Cards.

FOUR TIMES DEBIT CARDS ARE DEPICTED IN THE BOOK. EACH TIME THE CARD USES A BAR CODE; NO NAME, NO ADDRESS, ETC.

The book explains among many things:

• "Your employer or a government agency can require you to receive your salary or a government benefit by electronic transfer..."

• "You could lose all the money in your account plus your maximum overdraft line of credit if you do not report an unauthorized transfer... within 60 days after the statement is mailed to you..."

• "You could lose as much as $500 if you do not tell the card issuer within 2 business days after learning of loss or theft (of card)."

The Federal Reserve System depicts Alice and her Debit Card, with her Bar Code, and the invitation, "use me."

tional. THE DEBIT CARD SEGMENT OF EFT IS INHERENTLY DANGEROUS. Not only does it eliminate all credit in one swoop, but it institutes "irreversibility" to each financial transaction. There will no longer be the STOP-PAYMENT privilege we enjoy in check writing when merchandise is damaged or unacceptable to us, and the merchant is obstinate. What a convenience to stores! No wonder they are working for its enactment! They, not we, will have the last say when a material looks like a second, or if the watch was or was not running when it was purchased. "The customer is always right" will never be heard again in the halls of commerce.

At the Mercy of the System

For years Credit Card thieves have been smarter than those who designed the program. People, with one stolen Card and a false driver's license would open bank accounts for a few hundred dollars, and go out and write thousands of dollars in checks. In large cities Credit Card criminals (many times ex-employees of banks, Credit Card companies and computer technicians) operate in high style selling counterfeit Cards, national data bank credit rating, and bilk the System for millions; for which, of course, the honest must compensate. But, the publicity these acts receive is kept very low key for obvious reasons; to not advertise the ease with which this can be done; and to not cast dispersions upon the System . . . it must march on!

However, the Credit Card fraud is a pittance compared to what can be perpetrated upon us in the Debit Card System of EFT.

"Within electronic funds transfer the possibility exists for imaginative fraud so massive that by the time it is detected, the perpetrators could be too rich to prosecute."[16]

Beside the absoulte loss of control over our money, there is

134

the — not invasion — but, elimination of ALL privacy; and the potential loss of everything due to computer thievery and computer error.

The overriding, overwhelming objection to this system is, however, the ability of the Federal Government to constantly monitor one's every move without the courtesy of being notified. It does not take long to understand whoever may have received credit for instigating EFT originally, the Feds helped promote it! No more will they be required to subpoena selective income tax information, for every thing about one's finances will be at their fingertips; how many people you took to dinner on a certain evening, what they ate, whom you called while at the restaurant's number, etc. Oh yes, if we could depend upon an honest Government which would never repress Christianity, we could breathe a little easier; but, Christians remember Rome. I walked among the catacombs, and viewed the remains of an estimated four million Christians who lived and died under a Government System; a type of, but less evil than this last Global Government System we know is now forming ... It will be the consumation of all evil, and its leader, the World Dictator, antichrist, will be the embodiment of corruption, and he will *"make war against the saints and overcome them ..." Daniel 7:21; Revelation 13:7.*

So, to see beyond our nose is to know increased government power at any age is dangerous, but much more so now when we see the End-time approaching, and know all government-owned information will be accessible to the World Government to which all nations are already yielding their power.

Big Brother was taken care of in the *Bank Secrecy Act. As one witness testified before the EFT Commission, and whose testimony was published by the United States Printing Office:

> "It is a fact that a large portion of the consumer information which banks are legally required to maintain is kept for one purpose only — access by the Federal Government. The primary example of this is, of course, The Bank Secrecy Act ... The Bank Secrecy

.... government even in its best state, is but a necessary evil; in its worst state, an intolerable one.

— THOMAS PAINE

Act makes it difficult to safeguard the privacy of financial transaction information by requiring substantial collection, storage, and reporting of individual financial transaction information ... If a Government agency seeks access to an individual's records from his bank, NEITHER THE GOVERNMENT NOR THE BANK IS UNDER OBLIGATION TO INFORM THE INDIVIDUAL OF THIS ACTION. Even if a bank wishes to protect the privacy of its customers' record, it is not able to guarantee that those records will be protected from Government access." Later in the same report we read: "Further, the Commission recommends that EFT systems should not be used for SURVEILLANCE OF INDIVIDUALS, EITHER AS TO THEIR PHYSICAL LOCATION OR PATTERNS OF BEHAVIOR."[17]

•This chapter uses the popular name, "Bank Secrecy Act," to refer to Pub. L. 91-508, Title I, 84 Stat. 1114 et seq., 12 U.S.C. Sections 1829b, 1951-1959 and the Currency and Foreign Transactions Reporting Act, Pub. L. 91-508, Title II, 84 Stat. 118 et seq., 31 U.S.C. Sections 1051-1122.

In one rather "typical" bank document consisting of two full pages a few conditions pertinent to our discussion are pointed out:

"Disclosure of Terms and Conditions of
Electronic Fund Transfer"
(City & County Bank of Roane County, Kingston, TN)

"4. ... AT PRESENT there is no limitation on the frequency of such transfers that may be made to or from your accounts with the Bank."

"5. AT THE PRESENT TIME City & County Bank of Roane County makes no charges to you for automatic transfer to or from your accounts with the Bank. In the event that any such charges are imposed IN THE FUTURE, you will receive a notice of such charges prior to their becoming effective."

"9. DISCLOSURE TO THIRD PARTIES: We will disclose information to third parties about your account or the transfer you make ... 3. IN ORDER TO COMPLY WITH GOVERNMENTAL AGENCY OR COURT ORDERS ..."

In another study done by the National Science Foundation for the U.S. Government on Electronic Funds Transfer in 1977, is stated:

"It is evident ... that the less/cash, less/check environment has the potential of placing in the hands of government far more power than in the past ... The existence of a UNIVERSAL IDENTIFICATION MECHANISM—applicable to a SINGLE INDIVIDUAL is a KEY FACTOR in the development of the INCREASED GOVERNMENT AUTHORITY ..."

When the "Universal Identification mechanism" for an individual becomes the only means by which he transacts business, one number will activate one central computer file which will hold all of one's data. Today, dozens of data banks are contained in offices around the country, from credit information, to medical information in hospitals, to income tax information with the Internal Revenue Service. Under EFT all the information systems will merge into one World-Wide data bank. Of course, one who now holds a Visa or MasterCard (for example), is already tied into a Worldwide electronic network.

Today it is still permissable to receive and use any number of Credit Cards. To lose one or have one stolen is usually no great catastrophe. Under EFT, when the Card is misplaced or lost, one cannot transact any business. How long it will take getting a replacement in a System where there is no competition (One Card), is anyone's guess.

Perhaps the wierdest scenario in EFT is that one could have all of his "Credit" drained without his knowing it, and the computer could be programmed to destroy all memory of the transaction. Computer thieves can in a few seconds embezzle millions ... in fact, the average theft from "on line" computer systems is $450,000. In the on line mode:

"The communication link is the most vulnerable to wiretapping. Wiretapping may be used passively to gather data such as PINs or volume of financial activity. It may also be used actively to falsify records, steal stored information on funds, or disrupt business activity by confusing records. Spoofer or imposter terminals are wiretapping devices. SPOOFERS ARE SIMPLE, INEXPENSIVE INSTRUMENTS THAT DECEIVE THE SYSTEM. A device that can simulate telephone company tones and control codes is an example of a spoofer. Although spoofers and imposter terminals function on similar principles, the imposter terminal is more complex and expensive than the spoofer. Its potential for penetrating and manipulating the EFT System is much greater because it appears to the System to be a valid terminal."[18]

Finally, the industry admits that not only programmers make errors, but estimates of computer error vary from 1 to 7%. With 220 million people in the United States alone, there is the possibility that 15,400,000 could lose some-to-all of their purchasing (transfer) privilege.

Many cases involve entry of false information, about which most of us could never learn, but from which we could suffer much unjustly. Incorrect data could be entered by error or by intent. One such case rather widely acclaimed illustrates the point well:

> A divorced lady in the mid-west discovered information had been entered in her "financial file" which was transmitted to an insurance company to which she had applied for coverage. She said that the information claiming that she had lived with a man, "without benefit of matrimony" was embarrassing, damaging, and untrue. A Federal Jury agreed, and awarded her $250,000.

It is highly doubtful that many of us could ever learn all that the System has gathered about us. A Public Television Program, September 27, 1981, on Invasion of Privacy with EFT, indicated that if we were to begin to try to find out all data about us, it would involve writing over 900 agencies for release of all of it, although the agencies share a common interrogation System.

In the book, *The Fountain Pen Conspiracy*, by Jonathan Kwitny, who writes for the *Wall Street Journal*, it is made quite obvious that banks dealing with EFT are outsmarted time and again by imaginative embezzlers, many of whom build or operate the System. Two hundred million non-existent dollars had been honored by banks before the fraud was exposed in the Bank of Sark epic.

Three persons were charged with transferring $2,000,000 from the First National City Bank of New York to First National Bank of New Jersey into a company account using aliases. Literally hundreds of such cases have occurred.

Most of us would probably agree with the assessment of the Card's Industry's Mr. Frank Annunzio who stated in a Chicago meeting in 1977:

> "I find the talk of a Universal All-Purpose Card a bit frightening. If I were to receive a card tomorrow which would allow merchants to access my checking account, permit withdrawals at cash machines, and an automatic line of credit, I would do only one thing — cut the card up into twenty-five little pieces and send it back to the bank."

This is sort of what computer Scientist, Dr. Patrick Fisher says that he will do with his "Final Card" when it arrives. "I am prepared," he says, "to return it."

This entire Electronic Funds Transfer System is a "means of MASSIVE SURVEILLANCE of the population," warned Art Bushkin, official of the Commerce Department, *who added, "by 1984 the system will be common." Chicago Tribune,* August 2, 1979, page 8.

Our Government admitted it!

Please remember! EFT is not only a Cashless, Paperless and Proofless System; it is a Control System. When we only have EFT, one cannot buy so much as a writing tablet on which to write an anonymous letter without the System's being able to track that name brand tablet to the store which recorded the purchase via a Point of Sale Terminal which spells it all out on the print-out and connects it with your Card. When only POS Terminals are utilized, surveillance becomes an exacting science. A widely circulated "daily surveillance" sheet might read like this:

"DAILY SURVEILLANCE SHEET—CONFIDENTIAL—July 13, 1984. SUBJECT: John Q. Public, 4 Home Street, Anywhere, USA. Male, Age 40, Married, Electrical Engineer.

PURCHASES: Wall Street Journal, $1.00; Breakfast, $2.25; Gasoline, $6.00; Phone (111-1234), $.25; Phone (222-5678), $.25. Lunch, $4.00; Cocktail, $1.50; Bank (cash withdrawal), $200.00; Lingerie, $135.67; Phone (111-8769), $.85; Phone (869-1111), $.80; Bourbon, $12.53; Boston Globe, $.50.

COMPUTER ANALYSIS

Owns stock (90 percent probability).

Heavy starch breakfast — probably overweight.

Bought $6.00 gasoline. Owns VW. So far this week subject has bought $25.00 worth of gasoline. Obviously doing something besides driving 9 miles to work.

Bought gasoline at 7:57 at gas station 6 miles from work. Subject probably late for work. Third such occurrence this week.

Phone No. 111-1234 belongs to Joe Book. Book was arrested for illegal book making in 1970, 1978 and 1982. No convictions.

Phone No. 222-5678 belongs to expensive men's barber shop specializing in hair restoration.

Drinks during lunch.

Withdrew $200.00 cash. Very unusual since all legal purchases can be made using **Uniform Federal Funds Transfer Card.** Cash usually **used for illegal purchases.**

Bought very expensive lingerie. Not his wife's size.

Phone No. 111-8769 belongs to Jane Doe.

Phone No. 869-1111. Reservation for Las Vegas (without wife). Third trip in last three months to Las Vegas (without wife). No job related firms in Las Vegas. Will scan file to see if anyone else has gone to Las Vegas at the same time and compare to subject's phone call numbers.

Purchased Bourbon. Third bottle this month. Either heavy drinker or much entertaining.

OVERALL ANALYSIS

Subject left work at 4:00 **P.M.** since he purchased Bourbon 1 mile from **his job at 4:10 P.M.** (opposite direction from his house).

Subject bought newspaper at 6:30 near his house. **Unaccountable** 2.5 hours.

Subject made 3 purchases today from young blondes. (Statistical 1 chance in 78.) Probably has weakness for young blondes. (Jane Doe is a young blonde.)"

Reprinted with permission from *Computers & People*, **Volume 24. Copyrighted (1975) by and published by Berkeley Enterprises, Inc., 815 Washington Street, Newtonville, Massachusetts 02160.**

Identification Implanted?

We are watching trial balloons floating in the EFT environment all about us. Only the advantages are usually propounded upon. Typical is:

> "I-V IDs? If Vern Taylor's idea ever takes hold, you'll never again be needled for misplacing your ID. The Colorado inventor has come up with an ID Card printed on a micro-computer chip that could be implanted inside your body. Once the chip is injected under the skin, the vital stats could be read by electronic scanner. Taylor thinks the implant would be perfect for driver's licenses and other forms of official identification ..."[19]

It is worth mentioning here that Revelation 13:16 of the King James Version says this "Mark" is to be "in" not "on" the hand or forehead. In researching every available translation, I discovered the New English Version says the Mark will be required in both places, the hand "AND" the forehead ... people could lose their hands. Oh well ...

Gail Pitts did an excellent article on this invention which could have far reaching ramifications. It was published in the *Denver Post*, June 21, 1981. Let us examine some of her findings which she captions:

> Chip Implant May Replace ID Card
> "It's finally happening: the ALL PURPOSE IDENTIFI-CATION computer chip for ANIMALS, PEOPLE, heavy equipment, and the daily TV set ... a chip ... about the diameter of the lead in an automatic pencil — which can be injected with a simple insulin-type syringe into HU-MAN or horse ... the needle is capped and READY TO FOREVER IDENTIFY SOMETHING — OR SOME-BODY. ... It can be fixed to inanimate objects with epoxy — hidden inside a TV set ... or under the felt on the base of an antique silver candlestick ... Contained

in the package is an induction coil and a capacitor to create a weak electrical signal when a scanner activates it. ... One wafer is encoded with a **12-DIGIT** unique Number. WITH 12 DIGITS, THE SYSTEM CAN PRODUCE SOME 4 BILLION UNIQUE NUMBERS."

My asssessment is that Identification will sequentially be via a Card with a Bar Code Encodation of one's Number, plus photograph and signature. However, the Government is obviously very interested in INSTANTANEOUS IDENTIFICATION as the article states:

"SYSTEM ID's injected chip is the outgrowth of ELECTRONIC IDENTIFICATION RESEARCH conducted over the past 10 years by the FEDERAL GOVERNMENT at Las Alamos."

In this vein the chip would identify: whereabouts of all classes of people (President Reagan's would-be assassin is being electronically monitored in his cell); pets, leased equipment, the family car, cattle, etc. And, while it has many advantages, especially for the rancher, and scientists who could "watch" birds in their migratory environments, it could be the final step in implementing George Orwell's "1984."

The "Marked" Society

The "Marking" System which provides IDENTITY for single articles has moved into the container industry. Mr. William H. Wylie, Business Editor of the *Pittsburgh Press* writes:

"There's a warehouse in Kenilworth, N.J., that's seven stories tall and big enough to enclose two football fields. It's operated by three people ... On each carton there's a Bar Code Symbol which is read by an electronic scanner, or reader. The Code identifies the package for the computer. These little Symbols, which resemble a gridiron, enable computers to talk to packages and vice versa ... Use of Bar Codes has advanced more slowly in factories and warehouses. One problem was the large assortment of Codes. Every company was 'doing its own thing.' An automated system might work well within a corporation's plants, but not outside. A Universal Code, similar to the one adopted by the supermarket industry, was needed ... Earlier this year the committee approved two Codes. 'Both can be printed on corrugated packages and have a scannability rate of between 98 and 99 percent,' Field said. One Code is strictly numerical while the other includes letters and numbers for more complicated uses ... Other possible applications include Credit Card verification and movement of air freight and baggage."[20]

Note that:

1. "A Universal Code ... was needed." Little time is needed to count the advantages of a System which is compatible in every warehouse in every state, nation and world. Surely it is the most efficient System ever conceived. But, it has its disadvantages, not the least of which is, it replaces men who need to work, but whose wages have gone so high this alternative was found.

2. "One Code is strictly numerical while the other includes letters and numbers ..." The Wand (pencil like reader) CAN read numbers your eyes can read. A Sears Card, for example, has numbers inscribed on the strip on the back of the Card visible to the eye, and their scanner takes these off when purchase is made.

3. Letters are combined with numbers in some Codes.

144

4. "Other possible applications include Credit Card verification and movement of air freight and luggage." Credit Card Bar Codes we have discussed, but let us look at the Identification of luggage and air freight.

Luggage is "Marked"

STAPLE HERE

T A G   1 0

A Bar Code used by an Airline to Identify Luggage.

In addition, a yet more sophisticated System exists for monitoring a piece of luggage from the time and place it is loaded on a carrier to the time and place of its arrival, and indeed to the time of delivery to the owner.

The System works like this pictorially:

A transceiver is being attached to a piece of luggage which will transmit a continuous signal to the satellite.

The crossed antennae in orbit sweeping by microwave beam to cover the North American continent continuously, capable of locating any frequency within 300 feet with current technology.

We do not see any sinister application in this. One cannot help but realize that when available technology is capable of following an inanimate object; how much more human beings could be "watched" under a repressive regime ... and students of Bible Prophecy know that the most repressive regime the world will ever experience is converging upon us now ... this Global Cashless One World Order.

Farms are now identified by "Marks" in a Bar code.

DUE 7 DAYS AFTER RECEIPT OF FORM
U.S. CENSUS BUREAU REPORT –

FORM 78-A4
(12-9-77)

U.S. DEPARTMENT OF COMMERCE
BUREAU OF THE CENSUS   Form Approved: O.M.B. No. 41-S77090

1978 FARM AND RANCH *(Please correct any error in name and address including ZIP code)*
IDENTIFICATION SURVEY

NOTICE — Response to this inquiry is required by law (title 13, U.S. Code). By the same law YOUR REPORT TO THE CENSUS BUREAU IS CONFIDENTIAL. It may be seen only by sworn Census employees and may be used only for statistical purposes. Your report CANNOT be used for purposes of taxation, investigation, or regulation. The law also provides that copies retained in your files are immune from legal process.

CFN **71074-033920**   EI 00-0000000 0
                          00 00 00 0 0 12 0   4
00000000 0000 100 WASH 001 1 00

AIRBILL NUMBER
608427072

Federal Express identifies the location of each package via "reading" its Bar Code, within which is incorporated the Airbill Number.

Mail is "Marked"

NO POSTAGE
NECESSARY
IF MAILED
IN THE
UNITED STATES

BUSINESS REPLY MAIL

The United States Postal Department has "Marked" the envelopes . . .

Books are "Marked"

Grosse Pointe Public Library
Grosse Pointe, Michigan 48236

2 1226 00002 0228

SIGNATURE

The person whose signature appears above is responsible for all material borrowed on this card

This Public Library Card *IDENTIFIES* the *USER* by a Bar Code. No name and address appear on the Card; just a signature. Bar Codes are also used here to *IDENTIFY BOOKS*. Bar Codes for *BOOKS AND PEOPLE* are scanned by a laser pencil like reader.

The ISBN (International Standard Book Number) is a classic example of identifying each book in the future from the manufacturer to retailer to consumer. Within a short period, at the blink of an eye, a government computer can give a readout on every book sold, and to whom. If, for example, a governing entity desires to confiscate a book, say the Bible, the ISBN Number will have paved the way for the task to be simple.

Passports are "Marked"

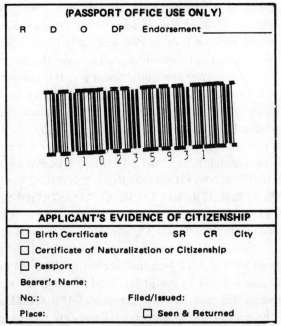

Passports are now identified by Bar Codes
Bar Code on Passport Application, as pictured in Department of State's "Travel Document Issuance System."

TDIS "WAND" Scans Bar Code for identification on Passport

Quoting from the foregoing TDIS explanation:

"The Travel Document Issuance System (TDIS), which has been under design for several years and under development for the past year, will be put into operation at the Washington Passport Agency in February 1981. Facilities are being designed for the Chicago and Los Angeles agencies, and they are scheduled for implementation in May and October 1981. The remaining sites will receive TDIS in 1982 and early 1983 . . . When an application is received by mail or over the counter, the first step after the initial sorting is the placement of a BAR CODE label (approximately one inch by two inches) in the upper right corner of the application. At the Data Entry station, the operator "WANDS" (with a laser pencil) the label which "OPENS" a record in the system for that PASSPORT NUMBER. THE PASSPORT NUMBER IS NEVER KEYED IN; IDENTIFICATION OF THE APPLICATION IS DONE AT ALL STATIONS BY "WANDING" THE BAR CODE LABEL. . . . The next step in the production flow is Adjudication. After the WANDING PROCESS, an adjudication format will be displayed on the CRT terminal screen . . . The operator places the book in the printer and WANDS the application. TDIS promises to bring many IMPROVEMENTS to the production of passports. Passports will be produced at less cost, will have faster throughput per book, **will meet** INTERNATIONAL MACHINE-READABLE STANDARDS, and will be less easily altered or falsified."

From the *Washington Post*, July 1, 1981, we see that:

"New passports issued in Washington are machine readable; this is the first step toward standardizing passports on a Worldwide basis."

From the *Bestletter*, October 30, 1981:

"Machines scrutinize your passport, then search their data banks to make sure you're of desirable character."

Thus we see our Passport Identity will also be a Bar Code, and our Identification will be "by wanding the Bar Code Label." As World citizens we shall have World Passports.

The Card is "Marked"
THE WORLD WIDE MONEYCARD
(The Personal Identification Transaction Card)

1981 Version

In early 1981, the essential information which I believed would be on the back of the Final Card was depicted on the cover of *"WHEN YOUR MONEY FAILS."* An article in that book on the subject serves as the historical backdrop for this discussion.

That we are coming to a Final Card is as certain as taxes. In the U.S. *News & World Report*, September 15, 1980, was an article entitled: "A National Identity Card?" The article indicated the U.S. Government was contemplating issuing this All Purpose Identity Card, without which a person would not be able to work or transact business of any kind.

"In 1798, a Methodist Minister, Adam Clarke wrote:
"The Mark of the Beast will be an 18 digit Number,
6+6+6."
Adam Clarke Unabridged Bible Commentary

In 1977, Dr. Hanrick Eldeman, Chief Analyst for the European Economic Community, announced that he was ready to begin assigning a Number to every person in the world; and that he "plans to use a three six-digital unit, 18 Numbers."[21]

In his article concerning the world's largest computer, February 1975, Mr. Charles Duncombe of CFN Information Network's Jerusalem Bureau states:

"Dr. Hanrick Eldeman, Chief Analyst of the Common Market Confederacy in Brussels, has revealed that a computerized restoration plan is already under way to straighten out world chaos. A crisis meeting in early 1974 brought together Common Market leaders, advisors and scientists at which time Dr. Eldeman unveiled 'THE BEAST.' It is a gigantic, three story, self-programming computer with the potential of NUMBERING EVERY HUMAN BEING ON EARTH."

Dr. Patrick Fisher, Eminent Computer Scientist, Consultant to Canada Super Conducting Corporation affiliated with McGill University, not only says,

"There's one more Card to come, and this Card is ready now;" but also that: "You and I are tied into this (beast) computer by one or more keys: our Social Security number, our driver's license, our birth certificate, our passport number, and whatever Credit Cards we use ... The computer capacity was set for 2 billion people four years ago. Basically, these were from the industrial trading nations ..."

When asked by interviewer to stress again that "every individual who is a member of one of these industrial nations is already in that computer in Brussels," Dr. Fisher replied:

> "Yes he is. And every move he's made, any change of address, what jobs, what his earning capacity has been, and what he has paid to the Internal Revenue at the end of each year ..."[22]

My Jewish brother, (a Christian), Dr. Harvey A. Smith, wrote in his book, "They're Rebuilding The Temple:"

> "Note the (Hebrew) numbers אאא (666). We are told to count the number of the beast (government) for it is the number of a man (ruler) ... and this man is the government. His number is (666) or $6+6+6=18$. The number 18 in Hebrew is signified as an "CHAI." It means "to live." (It is also interesting to note that this number is the number for the government in Jerusalem.) The "CHAI" pendant is a favorite work by Jews all over the world. It will also soon become the mark that the Antichrist may give to all his loyal subjects."[23]

**"666" Product Identification System
used by Koehring & Clark Equipment**

WORLD ID TRANSACTION CARD

6   6   6

2 0 5 4 1 9 3 8 6 9 6 8

AREA CODE   SOCIAL SECURITY NUMBER

(110 U.S. Code)
Magnetic Stripe

Mary Stewart Relfe
1400 South Decatur
Montgomery, AL 36104 U.S.A.
Signature

1982 Version of my own "PIT Card"

Photo—Computer verified via encodings
Signature—Computer verified via encodings
Hand Scan—Computer verified via encodings
666 World Code in Bar Code Encodation
110 USA Code in Mag Stripe Encoding
205 (Area Code) plus SS # 419-38-6968, (12-digit Bar Code Encodation)

I continue to foresee the use of 18 digits as has been projected earlier. I conjecture that only two of the six digital units (12 Numbers) will be visible to the naked eye. Their corresponding "Marks" will make up a Bar Code. The first six-digital unit will be encoded. As I see it, the World Code, a 3-digit Code "666" will be concealed in the Bar Code much as shown here. The National Code, the second 3-digit Code "110" will be concealed in the Magnetic Stripe.

In a speech, John J. Reynolds, President of Interbank Card Association, said that:

"The newly named MasterCard will be a full TRANS-

ACTION CARD, rather than just a Credit Card ... Even the NEW MAGNETIC STRIPE SPECIFICATION adopted for the MasterCard now EMBRACES an element introduced by Visa's **'THREE-DIGIT SERVICE CODE'** in the discretionary datafield of Track 2. With this Code, it will be possible to determine if a card **from one Country** may be used ... in another Country."[24]

This 3-digit Code which identifies Countries; (the U.S. is "110") is micro-encoded, but it is a part of the 18-digits necessary to identify each person. (I waited for issuance of the new MasterCard in 1980, and upon receiving mine noticed there was no additional 3-digit-Code embossed on the front. MasterCard had the same Number embossed as my Master Charge; thus the inclusion of it was not visible to the user.)

All the embossed Number on the front denotes is a file where data is stored. At the Central Data Bank all your many Numbers are merged into your Final ID Number which is coded ... When the Final Card is issued, expect only 12 digits to be visible to the naked eye. These will be your 9-digit Social Security, plus a 3-digit area code. There is talk of a new Social Security Number System; the 9-digit Zip has clouded the picture. It could be the new Social Security Number will be 12 digits. (A 12-digit Number has already been assigned to every individual in West Germany, and a Number is being assigned each person in Mexico, South Africa, and Nigeria.)

Also, notice I deleted "Money Card" for "Transaction Card." MasterCard is already a Transaction Card. Visa representatives speak of transactions also. Money Out-Transaction In.

Now the Bar Code construction discloses to the computer the manufacturer's continent. EAN uses a slightly different Set of Encodations for the European Symbol. The computer immediately recognizes the composition of the Bar Code and identifies the national origin. See page 61, (Scotland) Bar Code EAN prints out 12 digits. I believe the PIT CARD will in addition require, a signature, a photo, and a hand scan, all computer verified.

"These photographs were taken in the Saint Francis Catholic Hospital in Memphis after I learned that all business was conducted in the hospital by wanding Bar Codes. Patients and employees are assigned a Bar Code which incorporates their Social Security Number. Charges to patients and wages of employees are via wanding the Bar Code. I was taken into custody for having a camera in the hospital and was told pictures were forbidden." The Rev. Harold Kelly, Minister, Assemblies of the Lord Jesus Christ.

Three Distasteful Things

Solomon echoed the Lord's dislike with this straight forward talk:

"Six things doth the Lord hate . . ." Proverbs 6:16.

Here are a few the author observes equally distasteful in our SYSTEM:

1. THE MORE IMPORTANT THE ISSUE, THE GREATER THE SECRECY. Most journalists spend their time writing about strikers, or marchers or protestors whose actions are not worthy of being reported. But, they hardly ever inform the public of something so vital as the subtle acceptance of Electronic Funds Transfer, a System which will result in total slavery for mankind, an absolute "1984," a literal fulfillment of Revelation 13:7-8. When the EFT System is conducted with Debit Cards, one's every move can be traced . . . even to the minute he made it. While Christians do not have anything to hide from anyone, when the Government becomes more oppressive, and Christians will have to hold services "in private," the disadvantages become enormous. Think this not outrageous! Unless there is an immediate shift back toward decency, honesty, morality, and God, you will remember who told you first when you are singing hymns under your breath.

2. HOW CAN THE PUBLIC ACCESS THE RISKS OF EFT WHEN SO MUCH INFORMATION IS WITHHELD? There seems to be a conspiracy of silence. The few things mentioned in this chapter are only the tip of the iceberg. Most of the pertinent things remain part of the national or international treasure of secrets. Some of these are classified, others are just priced so exorbitantly, they are tantamount to classification.

3. WHENEVER THE "APPROVED PRESS" IS BEATING THEIR

DRUMS VEHEMENTLY ABOUT AN ISSUE WHICH HAS NO SUBSTANCE, LOOK 180° IN THE OTHER DIRECTION ... YOU WILL USUALLY DISCOVER THE "NEWSWORTHY" ITEMS. Harry Schultz, who owns many newspapers, and also holds the Guinness Book of World Records for being the most expensive economic-financial advisor in the world recently stated:

- **"PEOPLE ASSUME MOST OF THE NEWS ON TV,** radio and newspapers are factual accounts ... when in reality, up to 75% is often a GROSS DISTORTION, OUTRIGHT FICTION OR FALSE INFORMATION: furthermore, the big media in the U.S. is largely in the hands of the liberals, who usually report the most controversial part of a speech while ignoring 95% of what may be constructive talk."[25]

The High Costs

Satan is implementing this attack on two fronts, using first the desire of a group of international banking and corporate giants to gain control of the world's wealth; and secondly, the dishonesty of many unregenerated people to obtain something they have not earned. The second unit is working right into the hands of the first group, and will be used to convince the in-between sector, that Control by Electronic Funds Transfer is the only means of reestablishing and enforcing honesty at all levels. For, with it there will be no more cheating on income taxes; no more welfare fraud; no more cash-in-pocket, under table deals — for there will be no cash. All of the "Currency" of the world will be controlled by those who operate the EFT System. This group will at all times have access to all the money of the world. A person, reduced to a "Mark" on a Card, will have transferred from his account to say, a merchant's account, the cost of a purchase. Meanwhile, back at the ranch, those in control of the EFT System, which transfers this amount of value from the person's account "A" to the merchant's account "B" still controls and uses the money. It never went any place . . . they had it all the time. Numbers and amounts will be the only things shifted. The System controls both the person's account and the merchant's account. The most diabolical scheme ever perpetrated on mankind! And watch it come in on wings of acclaim from many sectors of society. "Eliminate Cash and you will eliminate 90% of crime," a spokesman for the American Bar Association recently said. No one would argue with the assessment, but it will eliminate all other freedoms we now enjoy. And, since there is a Freedom Connection, loss of Financial Freedom precedes loss of Personal Freedom. All of the programs designed to enforce EFT's financial transactions will result in the loss of all freedoms including our most cherished freedom, that of privacy. Mr. George Warfel states:

> "Within a few years (privacy) may cease to be thought of as a right, and a generation later, constant identification will be an accepted thing."[26,1]

> "In the case *United States v. Miller*, the Court's decision "retired almost all hope for a constitutionally protected right to financial privacy."[27]

Since the deadline is March 1982 for all United States banks to convert to the Mag Stripe, (*Business Week*, February 23, 1981,

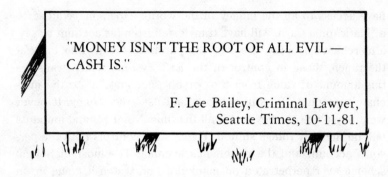

> "MONEY ISN'T THE ROOT OF ALL EVIL —
> CASH IS."
>
> F. Lee Bailey, Criminal Lawyer,
> Seattle Times, 10-11-81.

p. 107), there is still time to resist the "Marking" System for Cards.

The "Marks" (encoded information on magnetic strip), which now contain only pertinent financial data to which you obviously have no legal right — it belongs to the System — will in short order include life histories: financial, medical, physical and other data; and will be an open book to those who control the System, who will also control society.

I suggest that you examine your Cards! Request the former Cards used in impressionable machines. Defend the open System of the past, and insist that you do not want any Card that requires "Marking" in any way via Bar Codes or Encodings. By using a Card only for ID, paying with cash and checks (until money fails), and shopping in a less automated environment would send the most potent and intelligent message to the EFT System.

Christians, if Madalyn Murray O'Hare can single-handedly change the application of the constitution of the United States and thereby remove prayer from public schools, without the help of the Holy Spirit; what can a few thousand Christians do with the enabling of the Holy Spirit? FOR HE THAT IS WITHIN YOU IS GREATER THAN HE THAT IS IN Madalyn O'Hare. One Christian empowered by the Holy Spirit can put a thousand Madalyn O'Hare's to flight; two of you can put 10,000 Madalyn O'Hare's to flight. The old ship is not yet aground. Thousands of you Christians can lower the sails, let down the anchor, and altar the course of this voyage ... You can defer the enactment of this Satanic System ... if you dare to do it. I perceive there are many Esthers out there "brought to the kingdom for just such a time as this." I throw out the challenge to you, and remind you, whatever you do must be preceded by fervent prayer.

It is recorded that one person totally wrecked the economy of an entire nation during the Arab Administration. The economic devastation lasted for three and one-half years. Never under estimate the power of ONE PERSON-PLUS GOD. This combination is always a majority. The "God of Elijah" has not changed although I do not believe there are many "Elijahs of God."

I would not advise that you return all your Cards after March 1982. You may not be able to travel without one NOW. I recommend that you use cash and checks until money fails.

A South African friend, Robert Engelbrecht, purhcased a raincoat in a Penney's Department Store early in 1981, in the United States. The clerk refused to accept payment with American Express Traveler's checks. Upon being sent to the office, he was told that he could use the checks if he had a major Credit Card. He presented it, and they accepted his Traveler's Checks, which should be as good as cash. (Used to be.)

In Synopsis

Credit Cards are being used to transition us into the acceptance of the necessity of owning a Card. Whatever Card you now own will one day become a Debit Card with Personal Identification. WHEN THIS CARD IS ISSUED THE BAR CODE IDENTIFYING YOU ON THE CARD WILL BE THE SAME AS THE BAR CODE ON YOUR PASSPORT, YOUR LUGGAGE, YOUR MAIL, AND YOUR LIBRARY CARD. Then One Card will perform all these functions. It will be also, of course, the means of operating the Electronic Funds Transfer-Cashless-Marking Systems on our present course. Without a change in direction, by 1985 the world will be firmly entrenched in EFT. As the Currencies of the world become more and more worthless, EFT will be there with a Steady Value of Global Exchange to offer for the declining worth of paper currencies of the nations of the world.

However, our identity is fast coming down to a Bar Code. The numbers in the Bar Code will be represented by "Marks." The Prophet John would have been astute enough to delineate between a series of Numbers and a "Mark." He was and he did. He said the last World Dictator would "cause all ... to receive a Mark." But the wisdom and understanding necessary to identify this Mark, when it is required, will enable one to "count the number ... '666'." Revelation 13:16-18.

How long will we operate with our PIT CARD before some Great Innovative Thinker will offer to solve:

1. The problems of the lost and misplaced Cards?
2. The problems of the retarded and insane who can't handle their cards?
3. The problem of the aged and senile who forget their Cards?

For these solutions he will be hailed as the most ingenious thinker of modern time. The "Coded Information" now "Marked" on the Cards can be permanently stamped on the right hand or forehead. To qualify this statement:

A. *Navy Times*, August 4, 1980, reports the Department of Defense Department had received a bid to manufacture I.D. Cards for the military personnel which would **"use optical stripes (Marks) such as those** used in the Universal Product Code seen on grocery packages ..." and that these "will be hooked into a worldwide computer System."

(Military personnel have informed me that they are NOW being assigned Bar Codes.)

B. *Senior Scholastic Magazine* of September 20, 1973, pictures on their cover youths from over the world with Numbers etched on their forehead which would be the only means of buying and selling in the future Cashless System described in the article. See picture and write-up in the book, *WHEN YOUR MONEY FAILS*.

C. See picture of an ad in this book from the *Palo Alto Times*, March 3, 1981, depicting the future banking System being conducted with Numbers on the forehead.
D. See picture of ad with "Mark" in forehead.

This idea of conducting business with a Number in the hand or forehead is firmly entrenched in the mind of the industry, and will be the System "beyond" the Card on which research is now being done. Segments of our society are already being conditioned to accept Numbers on their hands for access control; for example, Disneyland in Anaheim, CA and the Pennsylvania Prison System.

After appearing on Channel 40 in Pittsburgh recently, a call came in from a lady who had been required to receive a Number on her hand, (invisible to the naked eye), to gain access to a part of the prison. It was by placing her hand under a light, that she was admitted and allowed to exit. She later became disturbed and felt this was not pleasing to God. We assured her that it was not the sin about which John spoke in Revelation 14:9-11. It was a precursor of the Mark of the Beast. And, even as we counselled with her, I feel now impressed to share with readers:

God forbids that his children "print any Marks upon them!" Leviticus 19:28. However, as I see this System developing, I foresee the insertion of "Numbers," or "Marks" (Coded Info) on persons' bodies first as "tests." (The I.D. Computer Cards for the military which began in Fiscal Year 1982 began as a six month test.) It is logical, and not without precedent, that it will be used first on helpless victims, as persons in mental institutions. It can then be assessed so successful that by the time the Jewish False Messiah, Mr. "666" is revealed, "he will cause ALL to receive a 'Mark'." In no way will the portent spoken of here be the Mark of the Beast; nor could anyone's actions ever determine the destiny of an irresponsible person. The unpardonable sin of the Mark of the Beast is more than receiving a Mark; **it is accepting a "Man as God; worshipping him and his image in place of God, and receiving his "Mark."** This is the subject of the Chapter, The Mark of The Beast.

Up to now, 1982, I have frequently remarked that: I didn't believe Christians should necessarily be independent of the Card Segment of the Electronic Money System. The Cards were, of course, as much more convenient over checks, as checks were over cash. I have always recommended Card purchases be paid up monthly, where one check could pay for, say, ten purchases. However, when I made those statements about the use of earlier Cards, I had not learned that Cards had been catapulted to the next and more ominous step prophetically, and were already being manufactured with Marks in or on them.

While we yet know in "part," we know "A part." Prophetic research, like any other, is line upon line, precept upon precept, here a little, there a little; and, as time marches on, these "parts" in the End-time scenario become more obvious. We grope for revelations which will enable us to advance from Part A to Part B, and drool when we read of the omniscience of God ... No one like unto Him, no one with whom He can be compared.

Oh, does the inquiring Spirit cry out:

"OH TO BE LIKE HIM,
OH TO BE LIKE HIM,
PRECIOUS REDEEMER, PURE as thou art;
Come in thy sweetness, Come in thy fullness,
STAMP thine own image—deep on my heart."

How encouraging to be able to intermittantly report some good news! Here it is. *"WHEN WE SHALL SEE HIM, WE SHALL BE LIKE HIM." I John 3:2.* And, according to the scenario I am viewing:

"IT WON'T BE LONG, TILL WE'LL BE GOING HOME."

Wouldn't it be sad if all I could write about had to do with Cards, Marks, Bar Codes and Money? If you haven't already discovered, you soon will; the underlying theme which flows out spontaneously from time to time is J-E-S-U-S, my wonderful, wonderful Lord. Get accustomed now to the intrusion. When He moves in, data moves out. The "letter" killeth, but the Spirit "Maketh alive." And, I already discern that the same Spirit which raised Jesus from the dead is quickening, sorting and selecting the topics. We are therefore assured that we are in for an exciting adventure. GOD IS NEVER THE AUTHOR OF BOREDOM. He is full of pleasant surprises at the most unexpected times. In fact, "in His presence there is 'fulness of joy, and at His right hand there are pleasures forever more'." Join me now! Let's be "pleasure seekers" in our search for God. "A merry heart doeth good like a medicine." We can medicate ourselves at any time! Satan or no Satan; System or no System, you will discover as I have that:

"Jesus, Jesus, Jesus, (is the)
Sweetest name I know,
(That He) Fills my every longing,
(And) Keeps me singing as I go.

The man who wrote this chorus, L. B. Bridgers, had just lost his wife and home in a fire. Few of us facing this System will ever lose more than he; yet few of us will ever rise in such victory that we can author so great a proclamation. So,

"Turn you eyes upon Jesus,
Look full in His wonderful face
And the THINGS OF THE WORLD — Money, Cards
Marks —
Will grow strangely dim,
In the light of His Glory and Grace!"
HALLELUJAH!

"Conditioning" Is On

"My number's right on the top of my head."

The First National Bank of Memphis, Tennessee, used this in their advertising recently. "ONLY YOU AND THE COMPUTER KNOW YOUR NUMBER."

Tattooist Cliff Raven etches a customer's Social Security number on his upper arm, reports the *Chicago Sun-Times*.

The First Tennessee Bank suggests the ease of remembering one's number by having it "ETCHED" on the arm.

Here is "Prophecy" in a picture. It appeared on the cover of an excellent magazine, *Dealerscope*, September 1980. It pictures an OBSOLETE CASH REGISTER CLOGGED WITH COB-WEBS FROM LACK OF USE, and shows stacks of computer receipts, the only evidence of "Buying and Selling" in this Cashless Society programmed for the '80s. Welcome!

CHAPTER III

"In the time of trouble He shall hide me in His pavilion." Psalms 27:5.

THE FOLLOW-UP SYSTEM

Our Cards are Marked. Our books are Marked. Our Passports are Marked. Our luggage is Marked. Our Mail is Marked. Over 13,000 companies manufacturing automotive accessories, toys, books and magazines, hardware, housewares, paint, records and tapes, health and beauty aids, plus food products are members of the Uniform Product Code Council, whose products are "Marked" with Bar Codes. These efforts to IDENTIFY everything which will carry many advantages will undermine all definitions of "old fashioned" privacy.

Privacy is generally associated with personal matters; our words, our doings, our travels. This Numbering-Marking System which our Society has entered makes no delineation between persons, places, or things, and will result in the elimination of not only personal privacy, but that of places and things also. As students of Bible Prophecy, we know ultimately the System will put a premium on persons, **but initially it will demonstrate efficiency by its ability to IDENTIFY and MONITOR every PLACE or THING, stationary or mobile.**

From the official brochure, The Universal Product Code, is the following:

"Purposes Of The UPC"

"The UPC can be used as a common identification system, when placed on purchase orders, bills of lading and invoices and printed on shipping containers."

Thus, we see by using this Common Identification-Numbering System, (the ten bold Numbers printed beneath the UPC Symbol), when used for ordering, shipping, invoicing and warehousing, it can become a means of constant surveillance of the item. Every case of say, Whole Kernel Corn, can be accounted for from point of manufacture to destination, where each individual can of Corn may be accounted for through P.O.S. Terminals; "Cash Register" print-outs to the owner of the Card who purchased them ... to even the minute of purchase.

Not only "Marked" manufactured items will come under the controlled status, but crops growing in the fields ARE ALREADY being monitored daily; analyzed; and the analysis is being disseminated within hours around the world.

WASHINGTON (AP) "The first link in what officials say will be a GLOBAL COMPUTER NETWORK carrying information about crops ... has been put into operation, the Agriculture Department said Wednesday. TODAY'S FARMERS HAVE AN URGENT NEED TO KNOW WHAT'S GOING ON IN THE WORLD'S AGRICULTURE.

What happens this morning in the United Kingdom or Brazil can have a big impact in prices this afternoon in Manhattan, Kansas, or Decatur, Ill. THE SYSTEM, CALLED THE GLOBAL ECONOMIC DATA EXCHANGE SYSTEM, EVENTUALLY WILL LINK ALL OVERSEAS AGRICULTURAL COUNSELORS AND ATTACHES TO DEPARTMENT ANALYSTS HERE. Other foreign hookups are expected to be made in the coming months and all of the department's 67 foreign stations are expected to be in the System by 1985, Smith said.

'With this System, any agricultural development of significance to the U.S. farmers or consumers can be reported and analyzed within a matter of hours,' Smith said. 'Information such as a freeze in the coffee growing areas of Columbia or an infestation of cotton-leaf worms in Egypt's cotton can be entered into our computerized data base so we have a daily, up-to-date picture of global supply and demand."

The hungry Third World Countries have been insisting on sharing a greater part of the United States food supply. This instant information will enable them to make their requests more specific. It is all part of the New Global Economics, pursued in the Ottawa and Cancun Summits.

Cancun, Mexico (AP) ... "A NEW INTERNATIONAL ECONOMIC ORDER which, in effect would transfer GLOBAL ECONOMIC decision-making FROM the industrial countries TO the Third World was being sought. ... During a break in the talks, Austrian Foreign Minister Willibald Pahr told reporters the Ministers had agreed in their first session that the Summit would concentrate on four issues: **FOOD PRODUCTION, WORLD TRADE, ENERGY SUPPLIES, and MONETARY REFORM** ... the Third World Leaders want a NEW INTERNATIONAL ECONOMIC ORDER THAT WOULD REDISTRIBUTE THE WORLD'S WEALTH."

Your 18-Digit Address

Identity of stationary places as homes, offices, and businesses is being accomplished through the 9-digit Zip Code. With the 5-digit Zip, a letter can now be delivered without city and state address, but street address is still needed. With 9-digits the need for an address for a location is eliminated. I expect the 9-digit Zip to be combined with the 9-digit Social Security Number to become **YOUR 18-DIGIT ADDRESS.** The Social Security Number will identify the person at that Zip Code. Thus my address would look like this:

419   386   968   (S.S.)
123   436   104   (Zip)

One way or another, our identity seems to require an 18-digit Number, as Dr. Hanrick Eldeman, Chief Analyst of the European Economic Community promised back in 1975 to each person in the world. He described it as "three six-digit units."

> "Whether the Mark of Antichrist is your own personal 9-DIGIT ZIP Code, or your SOCIAL SECURITY NUMBER, or an 18-NUMBER INTERNATIONAL MONEY CARD, only time will tell. The important thing is not the Number or Coding System that will produce the Mark. The important thing for all of us to realize is that we ARE ALREADY in the Age of the Mark. We are in the Age of the ANTICHRIST!"[1]

It is amusing to recall that when the Social Security Number was originally assigned, it was a "very personal Number." It was to be used only by the Social Security Administration, and information about it was to be kept confidential. It was not even to be shared with other Governmental agencies. It's the same approach the United States Census Department took in 1980 when they wanted to know how many bedrooms and baths were in a house; and what kind of vehicle you drove, and how far to work. "The info is confidential!" They assured us.

One can say that the Social Security Administration in 1972 had radically departed from its intentions in 1937. An official commenting on requirements to have a Social Security Number from age "6" said:

> "Such a System would further enable the Government to amass information on citizens and store it in a central computer under a single identification Number. TO DATE, NO ONE HAS SUGGESTED USING TATTOOS." Time, March 13, 1972.

The $300,000 Desk

There are some highly reputable companies which make "Security" their business: For example:

"For the executive who's concerned with security, Communication Control Systems of New York makes custom desk-top security consoles which would impress even the most jaded secret agent. The price tag for a unit ranges from $3,000 to almost $300,000, depending upon modifications. Telephone scramblers, wire-tap monitors, bug sensors, video monitors for a microwave remote surveillance system that covers 30 miles, infrared alarm systems, and lie detector equipment for both telephone and office are a few of the available operations. The firm also OFFERS A KIDNAP RECOVERY SYSTEM WHICH USES TRANSMITTERS HIDDEN IN WATCHES OR JEWELRY TO MONITOR YOUR WHEREABOUTS FROM A BASE STATION."[2]

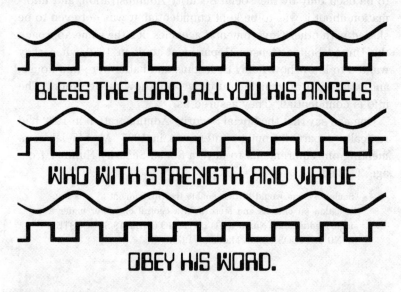

BLESS THE LORD, ALL YOU HIS ANGELS

WHO WITH STRENGTH AND VIRTUE

OBEY HIS WORD.

"These curved and castellated lines magnified many times represent 'one of the most important advances in decades.' Telephone conversations have heretofore travelled via analog transmissions, but conversations are now reduced to digital signals, as shown above. 'As the world's telephone systems follow our lead and convert to digital switching and transmissions, they will form a GLOBAL NETWORK OF SIMULTANEOUS VOICE and DATA communications.'" Northern Telecom, Business Week, September 21, 1981 Advertisement.

CHAPTER IV

NO PLACE TO HIDE

The "Marked" Society is only a part of the frightening aspects of the future. Simple, inexpensive technology exists that permit private conversations to be listened to secretly (though illegally) by anyone, anywhere, anytime. In addition, wireless microwave Systems permit VISUAL SURVEILLANCE. Simple looking wrist watches can pick up conversations up to thirty feet away and transmit them one and one-half miles away to be recorded.

As a student of Bible Prophecy for thirty years, I have believed that the ultimate tracking device used by the antichrist would be implanted under the skin. A Christian Computer Scientist indicated that the "Mark" a person will be ordered to receive could be composed of a substance capable of emitting one watt, which, he said, "would be amply sufficient for monitoring travel in a sophisticated surveillance System."

"Set a watch, O Lord, before my mouth; keep the door of my lips." Psalms 141:3

When the Psalmist wrote these words, he probably never perceived anyone other than God could become a Silent Listener to every private conversation. Neither could he have believed the time would come when a person would not be able to destroy a written message by burning it ... But,

173

Those were the days, my friend,
That abruptly came to an end,
With infrared.

"Even papers burned or stained beyond recognition can be transformed into the human range of visibility," writes an infrared detection System Representative.

The Supreme Court ruled in 1976, in the "United States versus Miller" case an individual had no "legal expectation of privacy."

Privacy is so relegated to the past that updated efforts are constantly being made to define it away. The problem is the definition seems to be left to the market place; to the industry, to the Government, and not to the individual. One economist has cut up privacy into three segments: 1) Personal Secrets to which no one (but everyone) is entitled; 2) Personal Seclusion to which one is entitled, and 3) Personal Anatomy.

"BID PRIVACY FAREWELL, because it is definitely on the way out. This is not your run of the mill threat from the CIA or the FBI, but an invasion of all you hold private by the new and inescapable information Managers."[1]

Mr. Robert Ellis Smith in the *Privacy Journal* states:

"More than one-half of all labor income is now earned by people involved in the information business."

Mr. John Koten, Staff Reporter for the Wall Street Journal asked:

"Has General Motors Corporation equipped some of its cars with devices to spy on drivers?' According to an electronics trade publication, the answer may be yes. GM acknowledges that the computer-controlled 'V8-6-4' engine on certain Cadillacs has the capacity to record some unusual information — but denies that it ever would use the data for nefarious purposes. 'Any suggestion that there is any equipment in our cars designed to spy on a driver is pure hogwash,' says a spokesman for GM's Cadillac Division."

Camera From Which You Can't Hide

The most ingenious device yet involves sensors, optics and electronics which transmit heat back to a supercold detector. These are called Forward Looking Infrared (FLIR) devices and they dispel all darkness! Fogs, clouds, earth, woods, "there's no way to hide from its roving eye."[1]

1. "After ten years of top secret research which was designed for military applications,"[2] the domestic market place has moved in. "It's the birth of a whole new world."[3]

2. "This device shows the oil level INSIDE steel storage tanks; ship wreck victims miles away, night-grazing elk, intruders in dark warehouses, beside the many military applications." An English friend has confided to me that FLIR devices are on the IRA guns in order that they might spot a person at night, who otherwise would be totally hidden.

As a pilot flies over, the images of people below come up instantly on his screen. Never think this is some crude representation. "The resolution on the best FLIR screens is better than on home television!"[4]

I have a conventional photograph of a wooded area, showing only woods. I have a photograph of the same area with a FLIR "camera" which reveals a man hiding in the woods.

The thing about this tremendous technology whose applications are not scratched by the foregoing is that in the hands of a kook, it will enable him to literally become a peeping tom; for "infrared binocular-like viewers will be in the stores by Christmas 1985, at prices below $1,000."[5] (1,2,3,4,5) YOU CAN RUN BUT YOU CAN'T HIDE FROM INFRARED, by Peter Michelmore, Next Magazine, June, 1981.

The New York Times, July 17, 1978, indicated that the CIA used infrared devices to spy on student antiwar demonstrators in the United States during the late 1960's. The spy satellites orbiting the earth at altitudes exceeding 100 miles, reported cameras were producing images so sharp that it could be determined on which side of the head a person parted his hair. That was technology of the sixties.

Technologies are merging and networks between systems are becoming established using telephone wires already installed. Vice President, Robert W. Johnson, of Burroughs says:

> "Technology is moving very fast. Only 20 years ago we first put a resistor on a piece of silicon. It cost $10 and replaced ten vacuum tubes. Now a $10 chip contains 100,000 components."

Words to explain the technological revolution which will drastically change the fiber of society are understatements before they are written. Edward Steinmuller of Stanford University said:

> "If the airlines had progressed as rapidly as this technology, the Concorde would be carrying half a million passengers at 20 million miles an hour for less than a penny apiece!"

No one can stop this onslaught, and with each new development, another set of definitions emerges for privacy. The only sector which will remain beyond invasion is the soul.

There is the Bar Code Marks designed to identify every manufactured item. There is the Card with a Personal Identification device to permit the exact identity of every person. There is the "electronic chip" for intramuscular injection. Then there are additional facilities to effect a "1984" style Big Brother System of follow-up.

While there are many advantages which accompany these technological marvels, about which you can read anywhere, there are inherent dangers about which you won't likely read, which could outweigh the benefits; such as computer wipe-out by theft or error; the elimination of privacy, and total control over our lives.

We can be sure that when Money is the Prime Mover, "womb to tomb" information will be marketed on every person in a Worldwide Network of Data Communications.

Mr. John Wicklein sums up these sentiments thusly:

> "The greatest potential disadvantage ... is that an authoritarian re-
> gime might use it to control our lives."[2] Mr. Wicklein concurs that
> the danger exists that a dictator may arise and control the commu-
> nication media and thereby control the people, and that grass root
> resistance must come from the people to protect themselves from an
> "authoritarian president, prime minister, or chairman."[3]

Many times contemplating the realities of "1984," I pray the words of Mr. H. F. Lyte:

> "Abide with me, fast falls the even tide;
> The darkness deepens, Lord with me abide:
> CHANGE and decay in all around I see,
> O THOU WHO CHANGEST NOT, ABIDE WITH ME."

CHAPTER V

THE REVOLUTION HAS BEGUN

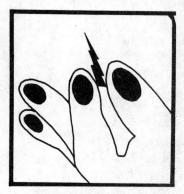

A $10 microprocessor . . . on a finger-tip. It is equal to a $500,000 room-sized computer of a few years ago.

Now! "Hundreds of thousands of transistors on a chip a mere 3.9 × 7.52 mm. So it's virtually an artificial brain." By Hitachi

It was the Industrial and French Revolution which formed the backdrop for the Romantic Age, in which seemingly looking for a way of escape the great English Poet Shelley wrote in his immortal, THE CLOUD:

> "I am the daughter of earth and water,
>   And the nursling of the sky;

178

> I pass through the pores of the oceans and shores,
> I CHANGE but I cannot die."

If the days of Shelley were characterized by "Change," events of today are accelerating so rapidly that no term of less scope than "revolution" could characterize our age. The revolution is in technology. This technology has produced the "Information Society," operated by computers which communicate with each other. A Miracle Society with unbelievably frightening aspects. For example, a statement is made in the book, *Electronic Nightmare*, that our telephone calls are now recorded. Vivian Horner of Warner Amex Cable said:

> "People don't think of the telephone as an invasion of privacy. Yet each call you make is recorded. When people get as used to two-way cable as to the telephone, they will take it as a matter of fact."[1]

Words are inadequate to describe the advances in computer and interactive technology of recent years. The tiny microprocessor, which fits on the tip of one's finger and costs less than $10 is equivalent to a computer which filled a room and cost $500,000 a few years back. And, these developments will soon be eclipsed by more powerful microcomputers; computers that according to Jim Eldin, Computer Scientist, "Can be **COMMANDED** rather than programmed." Computers costing $9 million today can be held in one's hand within three to five years.

The C2E2 Computer was called "one of the most advanced of its type" by Apple Magazine.

> "It turns on and off lights, radios or TV sets, types letters, answers the telephone, composes music ... etc. — all by VOICE COMMAND."[2]

This "Miracle" for the handicapped is made by a local firm, Industrial Technologies of Montgomery, Alabama.

Hitachi produces a "voice response System which lets a computer speak with a natural human voice."[3]

Then there is an electronic device for the telephone which "turns a woman's voice into a man, and a man's voice into something else entirely."[4] It was designed to discourage telephone harrassment.

An IBM official was sharing with me recently about the pico-processor which would be a million times more powerful and have molecular sized cirucits. One is designed to operate in the absence of any outside power source, being powered by self-contained hydraulic fluid which uses the molecular structure of the hydraulic compounds in which to store its information.

The far reaching effects of such technology are limited only by one's imaginations.

Issues worth thinking about:

- In the Futurist, Jon Roland, Computer Scientist, says: "More than half the occupations listed in the yellow pages of the telephone directory will cease to exist ... within the next few years."

- The Postal Service of the United States is not expected to survive the competition of ITT, AT&T, and others when mail goes "all electronic." One said that "it too will pass, as surely as the Pony Express." Sweden is already offering electronic mail between the Post Offices and major cities.

- "Welcome, Let's shake hands. Wow! What a grip!" An interesting comment you say, but hardly anything startling. Perhaps you'd be right if that were a human talking, but that quote came from 500 lbs of metal with a TV camera for eyes and an assortment of sophisticated sensors for brains—the Robot Sensor made by Matsushita Electric.

- Japan's stated goal is to have totally UNMANNED factories by 1985. These will be staffed with "robots which need no heat or air conditioning, take no breaks, don't complain, work 24 hours a day, need no time off for union meetings, and lift loads to 500 lbs."

  "Today's robots could replace one million workers by 1990 in the automotive, electrical-equipment, machinery and fabricated-metals industries, concluded a recent study by Carnegie-Mellon University. Robert Ayres, Engineering Professor at Carnegie-Mellon said: 'Some time after 1990, robot capabilities will be such as to make all (7.9 million) manufacturing operatives (in these industries) replaceable,' and three million jobs actually may be lost. Seeing the threat to jobs, union officials vow to make protection against robot invasion a top priority in bargaining next year."[5]

"Scientists are devising machines that can see, feel, hear, walk, make decisions, and reproduce themselves . . . robots may never look much like people, but they are evolving into a living species."[6]

Electronic "talking" devices are mass produced by Texas Instruments. One such product is a "Speak and Spell" game for youngsters. Others could soon provide hearing for the deaf and seeing for the blind.

"It is completely reasonable to expect that within twenty-five years electronics will be able to rival the retina of the human eye."[7]

• Bell Telephone is projecting . . . cordless phones and a NATIONAL TELEPHONE NUMBER for each individual."[8]

• Sweden's hard of hearing citizens will soon have telephones which print the text of a conversation.

• New televisions in Japan now turn on and off and change channels by voice command. These will be available shortly elsewhere. Meanwhile, the new "stylesetter TV shows how you'll look in a different hairstyle or with a moustache."[9]

• A new microwave oven can "respond to your verbal instructions, and announce in its own voice when the meal is completed."[10]

• "One thing is clear,: before the end of this decade, electronic voices will be squawking at people from all manner of everyday objects — including vacuum cleaners, washing machines and car dashboards."[11]

• The paper telephone directory is on the block. In France the telephone company is planning to replace it with an Antiope terminal. This is estimated to be a conservative move; replacing millions of paper directories a year for a one-time terminal.

- Cable TV, with its 2-way capabilities, estimated to have been in one in three households the beginning of 1982, may convert the home into a shopping center, bank, school, post office, library, or church; changing the basic structure of our lives, our work, our play, our education, and even our worship.

- In 1965 there were 3 programmers for each computer, by 1985 there will be 15 computers to each programmer. "As we have all become telephone operators, then, we will all become computer programmers."[12]

xxxxxxxxxxxxxxxxxxxxxxxxxxxxxxxxxxxxxxxxxxxxxxxxxxxu

CHAPTER VI

THE MONEY PROBLEM

THE NEW 5¢ PIECE

Dr. Franz Pick, World Currency Authority, stated in June, 1981, *"The dollar is now approximately 4½ pennies of its 1940 value."*

Many highly intelligent people ranging from the Financial Editor of the London Times to hard-money economists, are predicting riot, revolution, and chaos resulting from hyperinflation due to the ever accelerating debts of the world. Government after government is at the point of bankruptcy; banks are poised on the brink of disaster; nations are lining up to default on re-payment of loans; huge corporations known for their stability, as General Motors are running out of cash; and the unbelievable news arrives: "OPEC could collapse."

> "LONDON—Sheik Ahmed Zaki Yamani, Saudi Arabia's oil minister, warned that a continuing decline in the Organization of Petroleum Exporting Countries' share of the world oil market would mean the collapse of the 13-nation organization." Wall Street Journal, September 8, 1981.

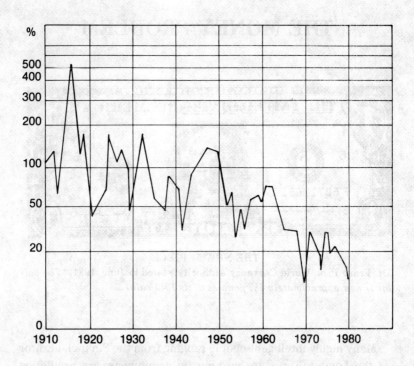

GENERAL MOTORS LIQUIDITY CRISIS
CASH RESERVE VERSUS CURRENT LIABILITY
Notice 1930 versus 1980. General Motors paid dividends from profits in the days of the Great Depression. In 1980, GM lost $762 million; during which time they had about 12¢ for each dollar of current debt. With the recession of 1981, GM faces a real liquidity crisis in 1982.

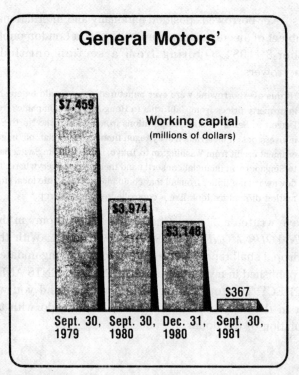

General Motors'

Working capital
(millions of dollars)

$7,459

$3,974

$3,748

$367

| Sept. 30, | Sept. 30, | Dec. 31, | Sept. 30, |
| 1979 | 1980 | 1980 | 1981 |

On September 30, 1979, GM had $7.5 billion in working capital. Two years later this fell to $367 million! In November, 1981, GM's credit classification slipped from AAA, to AA.

General Motors is however, in a better posture than say Ford, Chrysler, or International Harvester. In December 1981, International Harvester presented to the banks a $4.15 billion "refinancing" plan, the largest private debt ever "restructured." "Reschedule" will become the term both governments and businesses will use while the worth of currency after currency becomes nil.

The banks are no different. In 1960 for each $1.00 on deposit, banks retained 37¢. In 1980 for each $1.00 on deposit, only 10¢ was retained, the lowest ratio of this century. It is now being conjectured that the defaults WITHIN the United States will be of greater significance than those of the Lesser Developed Nations which we have so long feared.

This "over-borrowed" position nationally and internationally was the subject of an editorial in The Economist, a London publication, October 3, 1981. Quoting from a section entitled, "The Overborrowers:"

> "If this overborrowing were ever punctured, there would be crashes in property prices from California to Hong Kong, in companies from Detroit to Seoul, in state corporations from Milan to the North Sea, in overstocked materials from Oregon timber to Nigerian oil, in government credit from Washington to Tokyo, in banks from Switzerland to Singapore, in financial consortia and their clients everywhere. The downward multiplier from all that could make 1929's little local stock market difficulties look like a controlled parachute drop."

I have written a 30-page Chapter on the Economy in the book, *WHEN YOUR MONEY FAILS*, released in 1981. With that as a backdrop, I shall reprint some of the more exciting updates which were published in my Newsletter, CURRENT EVENTS AND BIBLE PROPHECY. The topics selected are not the kind you will read about in the "approved media." They have to do with the final repudiation of the dollar.

Updates From Current Events and Bible Prophecy Newsletters

"WHAT AILETH THEE NOW? . . . THOU ART FULL OF STIRS."
Isaiah 22:1-2.

• **FINAL REPUDIATION OF U.S. DOLLAR EMERGES.** The dollar remained strong in 1981 because of faith in the currency, not because of convertible assets. **The dollar's strength did not denote soundness.** Its posture could change overnight! Borrowers are not borrowing to expand, but to survive . . . to pay for inventories, wages, and old debts. Quoting from Jan.-Feb. Newsletter, 1981, "Interest rates will remain high for 1981 ... despite economist's saying they will be declining shortly." As huge as the money supply is, it is insufficient to accomodate the gargantuan government debt plus the economy. Stopping the growth of money suffocates the economy ... increasing it fuels inflation.

• Interest rates must continue high because: 1) If rates declined sharply, billions of dollar investments would be dumped, and the dollar would crash immediately. 2) U.S. Government must borrow big to service the debt, and interest rates are tied to demands on the money supply. Additionally, Big Oil borrowed big in '81.

• I see two trends developing; BOTH ARE PRECEDENTS, and will affect YOU, YOUR WAGES, AND YOUR WORTH.

I. The ever-increasing RESCHEDULING of foreign debts in default to Western Banks; and

II. The U.S. Government's RESCHEDULING and subsequent MORATORIUM on maturity of Treasury debt. Poland and Zaire are the first two nations to have defaulted on their loans. Poland has not paid interest on it's $27 billion debt in 4 quarters. The banks feverishly shuffled papers aware that: 1) They could not repo the country; 2) Classifying the loan in default would have put their funds below minimum operating levels; 3) Declaring default would not only call their own banks into bankruptcy, but would start a domino effect on other banks. They agreed to "reschedule" the interest payments of the last 4 quarters to be paid over the next 7½ years. In the meantime, Poland's economy is in shambles, and they, like Brazil, Turkey, Argentina, and others will never be able to pay the interest, not to mention reduce the principal. Our neighbor, Costa Rica devalued its currency by 42% in mid-August 1981, while announcing that it must "reschedule" payment of its foreign debts to regain its economic health. Wall Street Journal, August 14, 1981. In December 1981, the Argentine Peso "plunged to one-seventh of its value in January 1981." Business Week, December 7, 1981. In the same issue, Poland was seeking to "re-reschedule" what had been rescheduled in 1981 which they could not pay. It was reported Poland could not pay the English firm for printing their paper currency. The Poles have so little faith in their currency, they have been operating a "barter" society for months. However, it is not my purpose to have you focus upon the problems of one nation or one business, but focus upon the trend.

Meanwhile, under the Monetary Control Act of 1980, our Government may buy these debts, and pay for them ultimately by printing additional $'s . . . transferring the debt to the U.S. Taxpayer via hyperinflation.

Another step in the death of the dollar and the re-issuance of a new currency is becoming obvious in the:

> "repudiation process—rescheduling and placing moratoriums on maturing T-Bills, T-Notes, and T-bonds." Expect an unprecedented push to get savings into Treasury debt at high interest rates. Merrill Lynch ran ads in 22 large newspapers for 6 days in the Summer of '81; thousands responded. When sufficient amounts are in the coffers, expect a subtle announcement, say, Dan Rather on CBS Evening News: 'The Treasury has decided to reschedule the maturity of some Treasury debt.' No one pays much attention but look at the results:

> **"Treasury Bills**—Bills maturing 12/17/81, yielding 15.5% . . . *will now mature only on 3/17/82, and will yield a little more, maybe 16½%!* **Treasury Notes**—The 11⅜% notes maturing 12/15/81, yielding 15.75% . . . *will now mature 3/25/85 . . . But the original 11⅜% will not change!* **Treasury Bonds**—The 4½% bonds maturing in 1987, now yielding 6.09% . . . *will now mature way off in 1997 (a full 10 years later) . . . but the original 4½ interest rate may not be changed! The 7-1' bonds maturing in 1992, now yielding 13.04% . . . will now mature way off in the year 2005 . . . but, the original 7¼% interest will not change!*" The L. T. Patterson Strategy Letter, 9-30-81, P.O. Box 37432, Cincinnati, OH 45237, Year Subscription $149.95

In times of hyperinflation in Germany, the Deutsche Marks were used for wall paper. Here a housewife is starting a fire with the German Currency.

Dr. Franz Pick, noted Currenty Authority, said in June, 81:

"A storm is gathering around the dollar. We live in a make believe world. One day it will have to collapse. We will have a new currency. We will exchange at least 100 dollars for the new dollar." SILVER & GOLD REPORT, June 81.

Dr. Pick, Mr. Patterson, and others know that on June 1, 1981, an emergency meeting was held between Treasury Under Secretary Beryl Sprinkel and a group of key New York bond dealers who play a critical role in the marketing of Treasury debt. The meetings are continuing. Mr. Patterson, in summarizing data from these meetings says:

> "As I see it, we are entering Step 1 of the final process of *scuttling the dollar and reissuing a new currency* ... Here are the sequential steps: 1. Rescheduling of maturities of Treasury debt; 2. Indexing of interest to market rates; 3. A moratorium on maturity of Treasury debt; and 4. A call-in and Re-issuance of debt ... and REPUDIATION of the U.S. dollar."

When persons try to borrow on these instruments after such announcements, they will have less—to no marketability. Many will take great losses and retrieve whatever they can in order to become liquid again. These steps could take place in a period of time, or over one weekend.

Financial Chaos In The U.S.

While you slept on the night of September 30, 1981, the national debt limit was increased to $1.08 trillion. If one deposited a dollar a second for: Every minute of every hour of every day of every month of every year, it would take 32,000 years to amount to a trillion dollars.

The government's permanent borrowing authority is set at 400 billion. The limit has had to be increased 20 times since 1970. But that's just a tenth of the case, one piece in the scenario of U.S. financial chaos. A fish eye view of the total spectrum of actuarial debt is what spawns the terminal prognosis.

With all the budget cuts by Mr. Reagan, a move in the right direction, FY '82 will leave us with another record deficit to be financed at record high interest rates. Mr. Eric Balkan summed it up well, *"you can't bail out the Titanic with a thimble."*

190

DEBT OR LIABILITY ITEM	GROSS COST	YOUR SHARE
Public Debt	$ 971,000,000,000	$ 12,137
Accounts Payable	$ 129,000,000,000	$ 1,612
Undelivered Orders	$ 452,000,000,000	$ 5,650
Long Term Contracts	$ 20,000,000,000	$ 250
Loan and Credit Guarantees	$ 321,000,000,000	$ 4,012
Insurance Commitments	$ 2,219,000,000,000	$ 27,737
Annuity Programs	$ 6,900,000,000,000	$ 86,250
Unadjudicated Claims International Commitments & other Financial Obligations	$ 46,000,000,000	$ 575
TOTAL	$11,058,000,000,000	$138,223

Taxpayer's Liability Index (prepared by) National Taxpayers Union
325 Pennsylvania Avenue, S.E.
Washington, D.C. 20003

About half the $1 trillion public debt has a maturity of less than a year! This makes the Government the #1 borrower in the nation. Forty percent of circulating currency will be used by Uncle Sam, which will pit the Government against corporate borrowers for the money supply. Caught in the squeeze will be the continuing high interest rate, which has adverse effect upon the economy. Worse yet is when the Government borrows to service a debt made 5-35 years ago, this money (of which private enterprise is deprived), provides no goods or services! The resultant decline in the economy will mean even less income tax paid into the federal coffers, less Social Security taxes paid into the ailing system, and more unemployment compensation doled out.

To further complicate the picture, before the recent round of tax cuts was approved, a recognition surfaced of the need to re-build the government's revenue base immediately. One corporate attorney joyfully acknowledged his firm paid 42 million in taxes last year, but expected to pay nothing to 2 million next year.

The Big Risk: Money Market Funds

On September 15, 1981, a Money Market Fund matured, with which my Associate, Sally O'Brien was to be paid for property. A call was received that the payment would have to be deferred. This institution had put a 10-day moratorium on the maturity date. Miss O'Brien received her money two weeks later. This is only the tip of the iceburg.

In attempting to keep the government out of bankruptcy, many are feverishly working to induce the public into investing their funds into instruments either backed by the government, or into funds from which the government can borrow. Ever higher interest rates are being offered. HIGHER RATES MEAN HIGHER RISKS. The fund which has attracted most of the attention is the Money Market. These funds exploded from about 70 billion to 160 billion since Jan. '81 ... which already exceed the level of currency in circulation!

MONEY MARKET VS OTHER INVESTMENTS

MONEY MARKET FUNDS,	unregulated,	unsupervised,	uninsured, no reserve requirement	
BANK CDs & S&Ls,	regulated,	supervised,	insured to $100 thousand, some reserve required	
STOCK MARKET,	regulated,	supervised,	X	X
COMMODITIES MARKET,	regulated,	supervised,	X	X

Many companies are offering their version of Money Markets. Mastercard and Visa's offerings are on the way. Before you invest consider:

• An insured C.D. will pay within 1% of MMFs. Should the bank go broke, FDIC **could** manage thru channels (Treasury Department and Federal Reserve) to print additional fiat dollars, however worthless they may be, to pay off the insured portion.

• A Treasury Bill, Note or Bond, though I anticipate future "rescheduling and moratoriums" on maturity dates, is still backed by the government and eventually could yield some — to all of their face value.

Since God's word says, *"without knowledge people perish,"* and *"to whom much is given, much is required,"* I would like to prayerfully communicate to readers that you should quietly remove your investments from Money Market Funds. Solomon said there is *"wisdom in a multitude of counsellors,"* so I give you briefly the assessments of two of the worlds most astute financial advisers on the subject:

> "I declare that U.S. MMF's are a freak, a fluke, a phoney phenomenon as dangerous as tulip-mania of the last century ... one or more of the MMF's will probably go broke, which will either set off a chain reaction or at best stop dead new investments therein ... And don't think that (for example) Merrill Lynch is behind its own MMF. It's a separate company. Merrill Lynch doesn't have to bail out its MMF, and probably will not, and probably could not. MMF's are a sham ... I predict many people will not earn 15-17%, but will lose 30-60% of their capital on the primrose path of MMF's." The International Harry Schultz Letter; single copy $25, year subscription $258, HSL, 9-22-81, Xebex, P.O. Box 1303, New Canaan, CT 06840.

> "What is almost certain is that the coming market crash and financial panic will start unexpectedly and move with surprising speed ... In trying to identify the danger point, we have to look for an area of enormously popular investment that's inherently unstable and ... most important ... unregulated and without investor protection.

"We nominate the skyrocketing money fund industry as a likely candidate for disaster. A disaster that could bring the stock market and banking system down with it." International Moneyline, Julian Snyder, 9-21-81, 25 Broad Street, NY, NY 10004, 1 years subscription $282.

In times of hyperinflation, peole find a barter System much more convenient. One trades a "cow for a car." This is presently the situation in Poland.

"Kartuzy, Poland — Tobacco and alcohol are the best currencies nowadays ... Money no longer matters. This small town of 15,000 is surviving on barter. So, indeed is all of Poland ... When Miss D ... gets to work in the morning, there isn't any small talk about the weather, or last night's television. Conversations take the form of hard-bargaining — a discussion of who has been able to get items and what he wants in exchange for them ... Finance Minister Marian Krazak has warned: "The devolution of Poland into a barter society is our greatest problem. We must stop cigarettes from becoming money, and money from becoming worthless.'" Wall Street Journal, October 23, 1981, p. 1.

"The men who run the global corporations are the first in history with the organization, technology, money and ideology to make a credible try at managing the world as an integrated unit."

Barnet and Muller, *Global Reach*, p. 14.

Quoting from the keynote speech made to the Third Annual New York International Investment Seminar, 9-17-81, by Mr. Julian Snyder:

> "The highest real interest rates in 2000 years are slowly grinding the economy to powder while consumer spending and frothy speculation continues at high levels.
>
> "WE HAVE HAD A NEGATIVE YIELD CURVE ... THAT IS SHORT RATES HIGHER THAN LONG RATES ... FOR MORE THAN 2 YEARS NOW. THE LAST TIME THIS HAPPENED WAS IN 1928 AND 1929.
>
> "It is widely believed that the depression of the 1930's would not have been so deep had the Fed engaged in massive money creation. Consequently, there is no doubt about what Congress will want, what the Administration will agree to, and what the Federal Reserve will do AS THE SLIDE towards depression accelerates. WE WILL INEVITABLY see the greatest MONEY PRINTING IN OUR HISTORY, probably to be FOLLOWED BY THE GREATEST INFLATION ON A WORLD WIDE SCALE that has ever been seen on this PLANET. There is, of course, no guarantee that this inflation will prevent a depression ... As in Germany in the 1920's, recourse to the money printing presses in the 1980's will set the stage in this country for the SECOND COMING OF A HITLER."

I refer to the subject in my book, *WHEN YOUR MONEY FAILS*, published in January, 1981, for a comparison:

> "So we see the giant wheels of commerce grinding slowly to a halt as economy after economy succumbs to the innocent sounding term 'inflation.' It is not my purpose to criticize any person, official, or institution, just to inform you that it has been brought on mankind by greedy, power hungry governments, which have chosen the one method (debasing the currency), most misunderstood by the people to bring the economies to the brink of chaos."

Oh, that I could say that the glow is on the horizon, and better days are ahead. They are, but, not before they get worse.

"History's great inflations have almost always been followed by a dictator who promised among other things to restore the currency's value. Napoleon, Hitler and Mao Tse-tung all rode to power on the back of hyperinflation." Time, March 10, 1980. 'As I have said, there is a unique aspect about inflation in the 1980's; it is world wide in scope. I predict that: 1) The next development in the formation of the One World Government will be galloping inflation worldwide, followed in quick succession by hyperinflation. Inflations significant to historians of the past, as Rome, France, Germany and Hungary will be totally eclipsed by the inflation our world is about to experience. This hyperinflation will be the tool used to get peoples and nations to submit to the Electronic Money System.) 2. When the economies of the world start falling in domino fashion, there will be a person rising from the European Community to begin picking up the pieces. Unfortunately, he will not be another Sir Winston Churchill, or General Dwight Eisenhower, but Sir Satan Incarnate, Mr. 666, the "Other Christ.' "

"HOW NEAR WE MUST BE TO THE "REVEALING" OF THE ANTICHRIST WHEN ASTUTE, BUT SECULAR AUTHORITIES, IDENTIFY PRESENT CONDITIONS WHICH ARE SURE PRECURSORS TO THE RISE OF THIS 'SECOND HITLER.' "

Reflections: When I think of investments, I think of "providing ourselves with bags which wax not old." Luke 12:33. When I think of securities, I think of relationships with Jesus Christ which are *"without spot, or wrinkle, or any such thing"* — investments for eternity. But, more than 20 years ago, God called me into business, and explicitly guided me year after year into profitable investments. In 1978, He "quickened" me to begin sharing my learnings with Christians.

I have shared the precarious posture of the U.S. Government and that it can not remain a viable entity very long servicing this ever increasing debt . . . which is not to say it cannot function as a cripple almost indefinitely. I have cautioned about the almost certain future rescheduling and subsequent moratoriums on T-Bills, Bonds, and Notes, although these would have more value than most Money Market Funds in the ensuing crash.

I have warned of the position of the banking industry in the U.S. and abroad, although FDIC and FSLIC insured accounts could, if banks closed, under the 1980 Monetary Control Act, have dollars printed to cover some of the funds.

"When money failed in the land of Egypt (a type of sin or the world, in scripture) and in the land of Canaan, (type of homeland for God's people) all the Egyptians came to Joseph (a type of Christ) and said, Give us bread for why should we die in thy presence for the money faileth?" The Egyptians had to barter their cattle, land and selves to that world system. The children of Israel were given the GOOD of the land, ate the FAT of the land, and dwelt in the "BEST" part of the land. Genesis 47:15; 45:18, and 47:6. They had little to barter having given up everything, Genesis 45:20; but, wisdom to preserve food was given by God to one of them, Joseph, with which God preserved both the saved and the unsaved.

Both segments of society survived in Egypt; the children of God, the Israelites, and the children of the world, the Egyptians. But, WHAT A DIFFERENCE GOD MADE! His children ate the fat, while the Egyptians bartered their cattle, land, and finally themselves. The difference in surviving in the 80's will again be GOD.

As we observe the worth of the currencies of the world eroding from inflation, we can watch as the promoters of the Cashless System blend the world's currencies into one "international value." With the dollar, it is T-5¢ and counting. Most every other currency is suffering equally or worse from the terminal disease. It can't be long until all paper currencies of the world will not only be worthless, but replaced. It is just one of those "things which must come to pass" before the end. Luke 21:28. The New Money will not be like old currencies which one can see and feel, but Electronic Transactions of A VALUE EXCHANGE conducted with a "Mark." Revelation 13:16.

197

ONE WORLD TREATY WAITING IN WINGS. The Atlantic Union Treaty purports to "tie the Western alliance nations closer together with common economic, defense and foreign policies, eventually going so far as to have a COMMON CURRENCY and an INTERNATIONAL COURT SYSTEM." Spotlight, March 23, 1981.

DOUBLE COATED
TAPE NO. 666

SIX HUNDRED THREE SCORE
AND SIX

Sears

OFFICE USE ONLY
0066635

666 601 687 35001 KM

M 01500

0584

SHELL

M.P.

bankcard

VISA

4509 0012 3456 1810

VALK PRICE
07/80
J.P. WRIGHT

LIMTS END
06/81 VISA

bankcard

J. P. Wright

496 01 234 567890

J P WRIGHT

00/00   00/00

Journal fiction

666

Ladies Home Journal

Your new
JCPenney card

No of Cards Enclosed   Charge Account No

M12/   1   666 742 522 4   2

SIX HUNDRED THREE SCORE
AND SIX

Social Security Number | For Payroll Office Use Only

666

Form 4677 (1-76)

South Central Bell

YOUR SECRET PERSONAL IDENTIFICATION CODE

6661

This is your code. If you want to change it, mark through all four digits...

...and use the spaces below to write in the four digits you prefer to use.

South Carolina National
Member FDIC.

Sears
Sears, Roebuck and Co.
P48836697656666

Pacific Northwest Bell
503 485 3045F 666
72 02 131

National Car Rental | OFFERS SPECIAL RATES NATIONWIDE TO CLUB MEMBERS. RECAP NO. 6666666

CHAPTER VII

"And that no man might buy or sell, save he that had the Mark, or the Name of the beast, or the Number of his Name. Here is WISDOM. Let him that hath UNDERSTANDING count the Number of the beast; for it is the Number of a man; and his Number is Six hundred three score and six." Revelation 13:17 & 18.

SIX HUNDRED THREE SCORE AND SIX

Here is WISDOM. Let him that hath UNDERSTANDING COUNT. Solomon said, "WISDOM is the principal thing;" but, in the same verse he added: "With all thy getting get UNDERSTANDING."

Wisdom is a state of being. We could say it has a "passive" quality. Understanding is applied Wisdom ... it has an "active" quality. The person who has Understanding in this verse does something. He counts.

Historically, the Church has taught that people could conduct commerce only by receiving the "Mark" during this last seven year period. Revelation 13:17, however, lists three alternatives, two in addition to what the Church has taught:

1) The Mark (Christians cannot take it)
2) The Name of the Beast, (not recommended)
3) The Number of his Name. (Wisdom lies here).

Christians are already using the Number "666" with which to "Buy and Sell." Here is Wisdom. We recognize it ... we are not calling it something else ... We are not passing it off as mere "computer coincidence," or superstition. It is here, and it spells out the greatest fulfillment of Bible Prophecy since Israel became a Nation again in 1948. We are acting upon its urgent message. We are refilling our lamps with oil, and trimming the wicks. We are making sure our "hands are clean, our hearts pure." We are acting like we know Jesus Christ is about to come back to this earth for a Church that is "without spot or wrinkle or any such thing." We are "redeeming the time" in witnessing and being about our Father's business.

Let him that hath Understanding "count" the Number ... "666."

When I published information showing Credit Cards from J.C. Penney, Sears, Banks, Telephone Companies, etc., using the Code "666," questions poured in. "Should we use these Cards?" Unable to reply to these letters, I did an update in the Appendix of my first book. The gist I repeat again:

No Card, no check, no statement, no tag, no UPC, or Bar Code, incorporating the Number "666" is a sin to use or to pay. Neither can these applications be the "Mark of the Beast."

Hear ye O Christians! it is time for some astute delineations. There is nothing innately pernicious about this Number, as indeed most institutions using it are honestly endeavoring to become more efficient. Most usages of "666" are designations of regions, billing cycles, or processing Numbers. It is time, however, for Christianity to wake up and realize that never before in the recorded history of mankind has there been a mass usage of any trio of digits; never "111," "222," etc., until now, the time of the end, when man's Number "6" emerges in a trinity, '666."

At present, I see no difference in using a Number on a Credit Card, than using a Number on a Social Security Card. The Credit Card is one method of selectively **disbursing** one's earnings, which is yet voluntary; while the Social Security Card is the method by which one must **earn** his wages, and has been mandatory since 1937. Ideally, you should pay up Card purchases monthly, and strive to become debt free. I do and I am.

Soon, however, you will receive a Final Card and a Final Number. I conjecture it will be called something like "PIT CARD;" Personal Identification Transaction Card. But, it will be the Card which will be as mandatory in **distributing** your earnings as the Social Security Card is now in earning your wages. It will be the

Card by which you both **earn** and **distribute** your income, a type of Social Security (Transaction) Card.

One much smarter than I, Dr. Patrick Fisher, Computer Scientist, says that he is prepared to return his Final Card when it arrives. As we draw near this time, I believe that each of us will be confronted with that decision.

Wisdom is you have seen this emerging Cashless System identify with the frequent use of this Number "666." Since you recognize that it is the System over which the "Man of Sin" will soon rule, you will know to never receive in your body his "Mark."

For continuous exciting updates, we offer a Current Events/ Bible Prophecy Newsletter. See back of book coupons.

CHAPTER VIII

THE MARK OF THE BEAST

As surely as the re-establishment of the nation of Israel in 1948 became the FOCAL POINT of Prophecy Study in the past generation, so the "666 System," the Cashless Commerce of the end time, as prophesied by John, has become the FOCUS of Prophecy Study in this generation. Central to this System is the "Mark of the Beast." While Bible students have historically viewed this "Mark" with great fear and concern, it will be seen by the world as just another in a long series of logical and inevitable steps in conducting business.

The world will become so apostate that there will be a "Famine for the hearing of the Word of the Lord." Educational and Judicial Systems have so successfully diminished the importance of the Bible and Prayer, that a generation has grown up viewing the Bible as just another book. These people who have no respect for God's Word will accept the Mark of the Beast System as 21st Century Commerce, and hold those who refuse it as odd, square, "flat earth society" types.

Inasmuch as an understanding of this End-time Economy will be the key which unlocks other prophecies, political and religious; there exists a great need to simply define the term, "Mark of the Beast;" since this will be the means by which "Values" are exchanged, or business is conducted in this last Global Regime of this World Order. One unique aspect of this end time Commerce however, is it will entail worship. The streams of Politics, Religion and Economy will merge. There will be no more separation of Church and State.

Definition

The Mark of the Beast, THE ONLY UNPARDONABLE SIN SPECIFICALLY NAMED IN THE BIBLE, and the only sin for which God metes out a NAMED 4-FOLD PUNISHMENT, is:

1. RECEIVING OF ONE'S OWN VOLITION THE MARK (BRAND) IN THE RIGHT HAND OR FOREHEAD; which I believe will be a Bar Code facsimile incorporating a concealed use of "666," unintelligible to the eye, which will entitle one to all the benefits of "Man's Great Society," in exchange for:

2. WORSHIP OF THE BEAST (MAN) who claims to be God; and

3. WORSHIP OF HIS IMAGE.

The Sin of the Mark of the Beast is composed of three INDIVISBLE components: 1. Receiving the "Mark;" 2. PLUS willing worship of the Dictator; 3. PLUS willing worship of his Image. This negates the possibility of anyone's forcing damnation upon another. While one could theoretically force another to take this "Mark," no one could force another to worship the Beast and his Image which are integral parts, and prerequisites for the Sin. Prototype: Nebuchadnezzar and his Image, Daniel, Chapter 2. Decree for worship was given, but the Hebrew Children could not be "forced" to worship the King's Image. Since Salvation is of God, He is the AUTHOR and FINISHER of our faith. Antichrist can not therefore be the finisher! No man can pluck one out of God's hand—except that one himself.

Marks, inserted on people, similar to the "APPEARANCE" of the "Mark of the Beast," will probably be made available for "Buying and Selling," prior to the revealing of the antichrist; but, THE SIN OF THE MARK OF THE BEAST PER SE CANNOT BE COMMITTED UNTIL AFTER THE ANTICHRIST IS REVEALED.

The Sequence

Since the emphasis on fulfillment of Prophecy has shifted to the "666 System," the sequencing of the requirement to insert the "Mark" on people becomes crucial to our preparation spiritually and financially in these last days preceeding Christ's return to the earth.

The chronology of events look to me to be:

1. THE REVEALING OF THE ANTICHRIST. (II Thessalonians 2:3; Revelation 13:1). This cannot occur overnight. Whether one adheres to a Pre, Mid or Post Week Rapture, he will witness the rise of this person. The mass media will cover his rise to prominence. It will expedite his ascendancy, suggesting a shorter time than say, for Hitler, who had only radio, newspapers and newsreels. The alert Christian will be able to identify behavioral traits as deception, flateries, and much talk about Peace. Peace. (Daniel 11:21,24,32,36). Most conspicuous will be his superb diplomacy with the News Media. He will mediate the 7-Year Peace Treaty with the Jews to protect Israel which may take months or years. Only when this Covenant is finalized and signed will his identity positively be "revealed." This Treaty will start the last seven years of this Age, Daniel's 70th week.

2. THE WOUND BY WHICH HE IS SLAIN. (Revelation 13:3).

The words in the KJV, "wounded to death" mean "slain" in the Greek. Notice he comes on the scene in verse one, then is slain in verse three.

3. HIS "RESURRECTION;" ASCENSION OUT OF THE BOTTOMLESS PIT, (Revelation 17:8, 13:14).

4. HIS IMAGE MADE; the requirement by the False Prophet (World Church Head) for the world to erect an Image to the Beast which had the wound and did live, (Revelation 13:14). It appears the Image is a memorial to his resurrection.

5. "IT" (THE IMAGE) WILL CAUSE ALL TO RECEIVE THE "MARK" FOR THE PURPOSE OF "BUYING AND SELLING;" (Revelation 13:16). The "he" who "causes all" is without gender in Greek, and refers to the Image; the personification" of the Satanic Trinity. As "Uncle Sam" personifies the U.S. Government, the inaminate Image personifies this World Government Regime. When Uncle Sam says do something, it is the U.S. Government speaking. So, the Image will speak and cause those who don't worship the Beast to be killed, plus cause them to receive his Mark; or, the Image will do the dirty work.

• Remember the World Church Head, the False Prophet, will have the power to give LIFE (PNEUMA) to this Image. This is a "ghost type" of life; A FORM OF LIFE WHICH APPEARS ONLY ONCE IN ALL SCRIPTURE; a totally unique kind of existence, without precedent, and different from other Greek words denoting natural life of animals, as "PSUCHE;" or life God breathed into Adam, "CHAIYIM." (The False Prophet will with "lying wonders" pit his ability with God's and attempt to duplicate God's great miracles; as breathing life (?) into an Image for comparison with God's doing that with Adam; resurrecting the Man of Sin, as the counterpart of Christ's resurrection; calling fire down from Heaven to compare with the work of Elijah, and many more. The display will be so dazzling that if it were possible the very elect would be deceived. II Thessalonians 2:9; Matthew 24:24).

THE "MARK OF THE BEAST" per se cannot be received until after the Image is made by the people of the world. Since the Image is erected by the people, it cannot occur without the world being aware of it. Since the beast is wounded and healed before the Image is made, we are back to the "revealing" of the Beast, as our signal ... which is what Paul declared. II Thessalonians 2:3.

Thus we have:

1. The Revealing of the antichrist.
2. The Wounding of the antichrist.
3. The Resurrection of the antichrist.
4. The "Making" of the antichrist Image.
5. The Requirement to worship, and receive the antichrist's Mark.

Some electrifying events must occur before the sin of the Mark of the Beast can be committed; but, **THE EMBRYO OF THE ANTICHRIST'S MARKING SYSTEM IS WITH US. MANY PEOPLE ARE ALREADY "BUYING AND SELLING" USING ANTICHRIST'S NUMBER, "666." HIS SYSTEM IS ALREADY HERE! HIS NUMBER IS ALREADY IN USE! THE WORLD AWAITS ONLY THE "REVEALING" OF HIS IDENTITY.**

HISTORICALLY, it has been taught that the "Man" would rise first, institute the System, and activate the usage of his Number "666." Oh well, a lot of doctrines are being "weighed in the balances and found wanting," in the avalanche of fulfillment of Bible Prophecy.

Ten years ago no person could have perceived that the antichrist's System and Number would make their bold debut onto the world stage and there await the Man for whom they were designed. The Final Countdown for the revealing of the antichrist is, "T-minus late and counting."

Let Us Examine a Few Key Words

MARK: (CHARAGMA-GREEK) AN IMPRESS, STAMP, EN-GRAVING, BRAND, TATOO OF AN ENCODED DESIGN, UNINTELLIGIBLE TO THE NAKED EYE. Revelation 13:16.

THE "MARK" OF HIS NAME; the encoded design received in the right hand or forehead of a person will imply total allegiance to this World Dictator, and will be the only "legitimate" means of "Buying and Selling" in the Worldwide Cashless System the last seven years of this Age. The "Mark" of his Name will incorporate the use of his Number "666." Revelation 14:11; 13:16-18.

THE NUMBER OF HIS NAME; Revelation 13:17; 15:2. This Number is "666," (Revelation 13:18) and may be generally recognized, although its use will be encoded in a "Mark" for "Buying and Selling."

BEAST; (Zoon—Greek) A LIVING CREATURE; but, different from cattle designated in Greek at "BEHEMAH" and "CHEVA," etc., A HUMAN BEAST as II Peter 2:12; and Jude 10. THE LAST SUPER WORLD DICTATOR, empowered by Satan, False Messiah of the Jews, known as antichrist (plus several other terms) to Christianity, will ascend to center stage of world diplomacy by negotiating a 7-Year Peace Treaty with Israel, and rule the world the last 7 years of this Age. He will break the Treaty (Covenant) with the Jews after 3½ years, and attempt to exterminate them during Jacob's Trouble. Revelation 13:17; Daniel 9:27; Matthew 24:15-22. His 7-Year regime will be terminated at Armageddon by Christ, at which time this World Order will end. Christ will reign for the next 1000 years from Jerusalem.

The World Order Regime; the Satanic Trinity will be composed of:

1. Satan (the Dragon) the unseen person who empowers the;
2. Antichrist, the Jewish False Messiah, Mr. "666;" a human being, possessed by Satan, the Super World Dictator, the BEAST;

3. The False Prophet, The One World Church Leader who does all the miracles.

CHAPTER IX

THE EUROPEAN ECONOMIC COMMUNITY

European Economic Community Capital in Brussels, Belgium. It was built in the shape of a cross. A new Caesar of the newly Revived Roman Empire, the "undisputed economic leader," Mr. "666," could reign from this building.

There is no way to overstate the prophetic significance of Greece becoming the tenth nation (toe/horn of Daniel 2 & 7) in the EEC, January 1, 1981. Each succeeding World Kingdom from Babylon, (the head of gold), to Persia, (the chest of silver), to Greece, (trunk of brass), to Rome, (legs of iron) to these Ten Revived Roman Empire Nations (toes of iron and clay) evolved from one into the next. The anatomy of Nebuchadnezzar's image depicting these empires comes to an abrupt end with the toes. Analogously, the termination of temporal empires will come to an abrupt cessation when *"in the days of these (ten) kings shall the God of heaven set up a kingdom, which shall never be destroyed: and the kingdom shall not be left to other people, but it shall . . . consume all these kingdoms, and it shall stand forever." Daniel 2:44.*

Notice that the Ten Revived Roman Empire Nations will not be left to other people, as Babylon was left to be swallowed up by Persia, Persia by Greece, Greece by Rome, Rome by the Ten Revived Empire Nations, but during the tenure of these ten kings God will set up His Kingdom **not to be left** to any other temporal successor, and it shall stand forever. We are witnessing the development and formation of the world's last empire . . . We are in the TOES OF THIS WORLD'S CIVILIZATION; not withstanding, we shall probably see an enlargement in area resulting from mergers, and dissolution of national boundaries, as we observe the final geographical balancing act, emerging in these final ten major European divisions.

Further clarification of this Ten Nation Confederacy is made by Daniel in Chapter 7. Four beasts represent these same four empires, but the fourth beast, Rome, in Verse 7 has ten horns (kings) . . . and *"there came up among them another little horn (Verse 8)."* This eleventh king to rise up among the Ten Nation Confederacy is the False Messiah, the antichrist, Mr. 666, who will "make war with the saints and overcome them, and power will be given him over all kindreds, tongues, and nations, and all that dwell upon the earth shall worship him, whose names are not written in the book of life . . ." Revelation 13:7-8.

This confederation of European nations already accounts for over 50% of world import-export trade (the U.S. accounts for 15%); and has a GNP which exceeds the U.S. or Russia. Already their textbooks are being changed to remove national legends, cultural differences, and to re-orient patronage to Europe, not say, Germany or France.

In the Economist, October 3, 1981 is a full page advertisement of "EURO PAGES," a "YELLOW PAGES" for the Common Market Countries.

> "In September 1982, the first edition of EURO PAGES will be published. EURO PAGES will be the direct route to 140,000 contacts in over 450,000 industries of the EEC."

This Ten Nation Alliance has given us: The World Computer, (Brussels), the world headquarters for SWIFT, (Society for Worldwide Interbank Financial Transactions) or Electronic Fund Transfer; The World Currency (the European Currency Unit); and soon it will present to the world its "undisputed leader," the False Messiah, the other Christ. Both his name and his Worldwide System will conspicuously bear the numerical entity "666." Revelation 13:18.

1982
European Business
to have its own Passport.

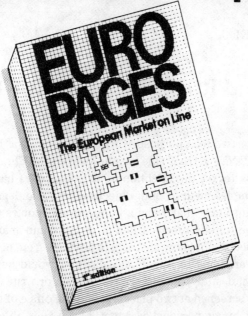

OCTOBER 3, 1981

THE ECONOMIST

LONDON, ENGLAND

CHAPTER X

FROM THE MAIL BAG

I had a two-fold purpose when I published the book, *WHEN YOUR MONEY FAILS*. One was to awaken the Christian, and the other was to get the attention of the unsaved. I have witnessed the accomplishment of both objectives to some degree.

I did not know that when a publication becomes a major best-seller, the author receives floods of calls and mail. I had pre-determined to not allow anything to keep me from my life of study and prayer. I had to refuse all calls, or I would have never had time to read, study, publish the Newsletter, or write this book. My mail was screened at two places; first at the office of the Publisher; secondly, by my personal assistant. I have been able to read only letters of those:

1. Who came to know the Lord as a result of reading the book;
2. That included substantial research articles;
3. Who asked sincere questions.

I wished that I could have answered the letters, but believe me, it was impossible. I had to learn to look at stacks of mail which I could neither read nor answer, but be satisfied just to pray for each person sincerely.

Thus far, I have maintained the posture of spending 60-80 hours a week in study. I feel that attempting to answer some of the most asked questions could be a means of instructing many. It's an old method; the Socratic Method, which deploys only questions in teaching.

THE MOST ASKED QUESTIONS

Why Not The King James Version?

QUESTION: Why did you not use only the King James Version in your book, *WHEN YOUR MONEY FAILS?* (One man judged me worthy of eternal damnation for this).

ANSWER: I study only the King James Version. I have memorized significant portions of the Bible, all from the KJV. However, "I am a part of all that I have seen," Ulysses said. My late husband was a physician who came to love the Lord, appreciate the Bible, and teach both Sunday School and Church Training at the First Baptist Church of Montgomery. **He could never understand the King James Version.** He majored in finding good translations other than the KJV. I conjectured that if my husband had a higher education than the average person, and he had problems with Elizabethan English, how about others? I did not write the book for theologians who, along with myself, cut our teeth on King James, but endeavored to use all versions with all people that I might win some. To those I offended, I am sorry. I believe the offense would be minimized if you could see the letters from those (including entire families) who have come to know the Lord. I wrote one man who criticized me: "How many have you won to Christ this year?" He didn't write again. I have learned whenever one stops to criticize, all forward progress ceases that moment. To attack, one must move backward or at best laterally. However, sincere suggestions, as opposed to criticism, have helped me much this past year.

What About Sadat?

QUESTION: What do you think about Egypt's President Sadat now that he is dead?

ANSWER: The same thing I thought about him while he lived. I said:

> The Number he chose
> On the Warship he rode
> Was an omen of things to come, "666."

Never have I spoken truer words. The name of the warship, OCTOBER 6, on that historic day in 1975 when he reopened the Suez Canal for commercial navigation omniously predicted the date of his assassination. I wrote an update on this subject in *WHEN YOUR MONEY FAILS*, and will only say here:

Indeed, it was after he rode the warship #666, that 6 years later on October 6, 6 of his countrymen would take his life. Later his **"procession was borne along October Sixth Avenue named for the October 6, 1973 Egyptian offensive that opened the last Arab-Israeli war."** Cairo (AP) 10/10/81.

I maintain Sadat is History's nearest prototype of the Jewish False Messiah! Few events in history equal the prophetic significance of Sadat's aligning Egypt with Israel, and thus engineering the Middle East Policy which sets the stage for Daniel's 70th Week. If we are close enough to the end of the age, Egypt will continue **"in league"** with Israel for Egypt is conspicuously missing in the nations which attack Israel in Ezekial 38, though historically Egypt has been Israel's most consistent foe. Furthermore, Egypt will become a dumping ground for the Jews during Jacob's Trouble, appearing to be their friend, but will turn on the **Jews (when great numbers are settled there, Isaiah 19:18-20), at the time of the very end and attempt to exterminate them. It is because of this deceit and abuse, Egypt will be cursed 40 years.** Ezekiel 29:9-15. I hold to these things: Sadat was the Prime Mover and Chief Architect of this end-time deception of the Jews. And, since he reversed his war policy against Israel, and reopened the Suez Canal in 1975, he has **"conspicuously identified"** with the number of Israel's False Messiah, "666."

Keep your eyes on Egypt, and its leader. This trap of deceit is set. The end time **"fierce King"** of Egypt, (Isaiah 19:4) who will have deceived the Jews into believing he is their friend, will wreak havoc on them during Jacob's Trouble. One day his deception will consummate in the embodiment of Deceit, the False Messiah, Mr. 666.

There is the other side of the coin. Israel's chief contributor to the "Peace Plan" with Egypt, Moshe Dayan, died ten days later on October 16, 1981. He was 66. It appears obvious that this plan to surrender large parts of the land of Israel to Egypt is not pleasing to God. Everytime Israel has been attacked, her borders have been enlarged ... by God.

Remember that those who get the victory over the antichrist (the False Messiah) will not sing a new song; (as the elders in Revelation 5:9), but **"the Song of Moses."** Revelation 15:2-3. This song is identified in Exodus 15, where Moses is singing about victory over Pharaoh — the first to enslave Israel. It appears that another Pharaoh will obviously be the last to enslave Israel.

Do You Have New Revelation?

QUESTION: Are you saying you have "New Revelation" for us today?

ANSWER: If I do not, I am a poor teacher, according to the Lord's words;

> *"Therefore every scribe (teacher) which is instructed unto the kingdom of heaven is like unto a man that is an householder, which bringeth forth out of his treasure things **new** and **old.**" Matthew 13:52.*

It is impossible for me to discern between Revelation of New Truth to me, and Rediscovery of Old Truth, (which may have been revealed to others, contemporaries or predecessors). I repeat again that the only thing about which I have received divine revelation, both through the word, and by supernatural confirmation, is the overall structuring of Daniel's 70th Week; the first 42 months being the Great Tribulation, and the last 42 months being the Wrath of God. I would be no better than Judas Iscariot if I betrayed the

Spirit of Truth who revealed it to me. Furthermore, this was not revealed to me to be kept to myself, although it took Holy Ghost boldness to declare it.

I taught a Pre-Trib Rapture for 25 years, and was so perturbed at those who had departed from the "Truth" that I "sat down" one day and determined to settle the question forever, for myself and others. I spent (God is my witness) 600-800 hours during a three month period; 7 days a week, living like a monk, researching only this subject, THE DAY OF THE LORD. At each point when I would disprove a teaching in Pre-Trib, I would get sicker, God is my witness! When the whole of the untruth was shown to me I was indeed a sick person; see Daniel 8:27.

About 80% of those writing me indicated that they had either already been shown this by the HOLY SPIRIT, or the puzzle fit together when they read it in the book, *WHEN YOUR MONEY FAILS*. Some have traveled many miles to say, "Thank you," for writing what God had already revealed to them — two from as far away as Africa.

Those disagreeing always confessed, "I was taught the other way." May I reiterate, FLESH and BLOOD (Mothers, fathers, ancestors) CANNOT REVEAL THIS TRUTH TO YOU, ONLY THE FATHER IN HEAVEN. Matthew 16:17. In the academic world, people's opinions vary widely in terms of competence. A person has no more right to an opinion he can not validate than a piece of merchandise for which he has not paid. "The value of an opinion can be measured in direct proportion to the price a person has paid for it." Dr. Thomas Lane Butts, Montgomery Advertiser, October 23, 1981.

An opinion and a revelation are two different things; but, I have discovered those who pay the price for the Truth (willing to express it when shown the Truth) are those to whom the Holy Spirit is revealing the Truth.

GUARANTEE: Anyone willing to set aside tradition, and allow the Holy Spirit to reveal the Truth, and "take the Bible apart" which requires time; the Holy Spirit will "show you (these) things to come." Anyone who sits down using guidelines laid out by any human being, will arrive at pre-determined conclusions. There are two disturbing aspects about this:

1. THE INHERENT DANGERS OF TEACHING ONLY A PRE-TRIB RAPTURE. When II Thessalonians 2:3 becomes a reality, and this Man of Sin is revealed, MANY "will come unglued." Plain logic demands presentation of the other views when there is an absence of a consensus among the brethren, and especially on a subject of such a magnitude as this. Unless a person has a Divine Revelation of the subject, the least which could be expected is that both views be presented. If the Mid and Post Week Rapture are in error, Praise God, we have all gained! If the Pre-Trib is in error, many will fall away ... indeed this contributes to the great falling away. II Thessalonians 2:3.

2. Twice I have been working in TV with "Big Names." In the first case this precious Evangelist confessed off set right out: "I read only your chapter on 'The Two Resurrections,' and I was convinced that there was something terribly wrong with what I had been taught, for I saw there would have to be another resurrection to accommodate Pre-Trib." In the second place, this "Big Name" confessed to me in a room full of people including my associate, Sally O'Brien, before going on live: "I believe the Rapture will take place as you wrote; but, I cannot teach it. *Our contributions would dry up.* But, since the subject needs to be taught, I am going to bring the subject up, and ask that you teach it."

What About Benjamin Creme?

QUESTION: What do you think of Benjamin Creme?

ANSWER: I think he can be found among those in Matthew 24:24, the second category.

"Benjamin Creme, a student of New Thought ... told an overflow crowd at the San Diego Woman's Club this week that 'the World Teacher' would declare himself publicly to all the world by

In honor of
THE DAY OF DECLARATION
Tara Center Presents
A Very Special Calendar

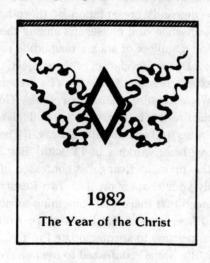

1982
The Year of the Christ

the Spring of 1982. Creme, a Scotsman, has been touring the United States to announce the coming of this New Age Messiah ... He will announce himself on a worldwide television hookup and everyone will hear him each in his own language ... This World Teacher will be accepted by Buddhists, Christian and Moslems as the one for whom they are waiting ... The burden of the World Teacher's efforts will be to convince people that there MUST BE A MORE EQUITABLE SHARING OF THE WORLD'S RE-SOURCES." (The Hunger Project is being advertised by the same people who have sponsored Creme's lectures.)

Creme said:
"He was aware that some fundamentalists would believe that a World Teacher preaching sharing and international cooperation was the antichrist ... The antichrist is in reality the energy and

222

destructive will of God. The teachings of these right wing Christians is meant to create fear. They don't want to see the change in economic structures. The change to the NEW AGE will be relatively peaceful, and Armageddon, the battle between good and evil that will precede the end in Biblical Prophecy has already been fought. The antichrist functioned through Hitler ..." Rita Gillmon, Staff Writer, The San Diego Union, August 29, 1981.

From Creme's own writings:

"By the Spring of 1982, the Christ will declare Himself. Look not for a religious teacher, but rather a modern man concerned with modern problems ... a practical man who is working through political, economic and social systems. Every world religion has a name for this Teacher. The Jews call Him the Messiah, the Christians the Christ, and the Buddhists the Maitreya Budda. His mission is to lead humanity into a new age. We are now entering such an age — THE AGE OF AQUARIUS." Spiritual Unity Movement, A message of Hope for Mankind, October 1981.

I hesitated to dignify this with a response, but Christians who supposedly believe God, and the Bible have expressed both on the phone and by letters their belief in this man's teachings. Two things worthy of mention:

1. He is "right on" with the subject that most touches Christians; hunger. But note that his organization is designated the Agency to TRANSFER THE WEALTH FROM THE RICH TO THE POOR. "New dog — Old trick" game.
2. He is obviously such a convincing speaker that, properly financed, he could stage the world's Greatest False Messiah saga via a world network. It has the potential of becoming the biggest cult yet.

Unfortunately, in times of crises, people historically migrate to the most vociferous, not to the most competent. Grasping at straws produces Hitlers. Leadership should not be based on oddities, or the new and mysterious. Walter Landon once said, "When little men cast long shadows it is a sure sign that the sun is setting."

Indeed the sun is setting. Many of our people educated in our Godless-Bibleless-Prayless-Educational System do not know enough about the Bible to discern truth from error. People are running to and fro to "hear from the Lord." Many will be deceived.

> *"Behold, the days come, saith the Lord God, that I will send a famine in the land, not a famine of bread, nor a thirst for water, but of hearing the words of the Lord: And they shall wander from sea to sea, and from the north even to the east, they shall run to and fro to seek the word of the Lord, and shall not find it." Amos 8:11-12.*

Mid-Week Rapture

QUESTION: Do you think your teaching on a "Mid-Week" Rapture is bringing about a disunity among the brethren?

ANSWER: I prefer to call it an awakening among the brethren. John the Baptist disturbed the traditionalists of his day ... so much that he had his head lifted. Jesus disturbed the Religionists of His day and they had Him killed. Truth plows a deep furrow, and people choose up sides. Unfortunately, most Religionists are uncomfortable with Truth. Every Order or Denomination which sets inflexible guidelines within which Bible subjects must be taught is circumventing the Holy Spirit from interpreting to the individual, and by disallowing free expression of that interpretation, is usurping the role of the Holy Spirit. While this seems like mass confusion to the natural mind, the Lord is the author of peace, and can be trusted. The true Brethren may split theological hairs many ways, but there is a great area of agreement around the Cardinal Truths; such as inerrancy of the Scriptures; the efficacy of the Blood of Christ; the Virgin Birth, the resurrection of Christ, the Ascension to the Father, the Second Coming, the Millennium Reign of Christ on earth, the Great White Judgement Throne; a heaven to gain and a hell to shun, etc.

Dr. Thomas E. Berry says:

> "General T.J. 'Stonewall' Jackson was perhaps the most brilliant 'attack' strategist in the Confederate army. It was on the evening of his last victory that he was fired on and fatally wounded by a patrol party of his own men who mistook him and his staff for a detachment of Union Calvary. Unfortunately, this is also a common occurrence for those in the Lord's army who turn their guns on one another and blast each other to the ground. As in the case of General 'Stonewall' Jackson, the results are often tragic. 'Many of us can remember how great leaders in the army of Christ achieved great victories against the real enemy until they turned their mighty guns on one another and blasted each other into ineffectiveness. They fell into the error of mistaking a soldier in their own army for the enemy. It is good to remember who the real enemy is.' "

Most Fearful Thing About End Times

QUESTION: What do you fear most about these end times?

ANSWER: Let me qualify "fear." I wish I could say, I fear nothing. But, Paul had fears: *"Without were fightings, within were fears." II Corinthians 7:8.* David obviously had more than butterflies when he faced the bear, the lion, the giant, Saul, and enemy armies. But, he said, *"what time I am afraid, I will trust in the Lord."*

1. Politically: I fear the converging One World (Global) Government, which will head up a World Church, and a World Commerce. Intellectuals are convincing in their arguments for it:

> "1931 ... There is no inevitability in the approaching catastrophe ... A few hundred million dollars for a world campaign for the New Order might still turn the destinies of mankind ... It needs only that the governments of the United States, Britain, France, Germany and Russia should get together in order to set up an effective CONTROL OF CURRENCY, CREDIT, PRODUCTION AND DISTRIBUTION; an effective 'DICTATORSHIP OR PROSPERITY' for the whole world. The other 60-old states would have to join in ..." H.G. Wells. (Note Japan was missing in the line up).

THE ABSOLUTE EVIL, an article appearing in the Bulletin of the Atomic Scientists, January, 1981, is described as being a reluctance to:

> "Get on with this New World Order. Another fatal cause may be that we have been so indolent if not timid, in pursuit of a New World Order where one can live without armaments." Hideki Yukawa, Professor of Physics at Kyota University.

The educational Systems of the world are teaching disrespect for nationalities, and allegiance to the World. On an international test given to 1000 seniors:

> "One way to move up this scale is to agree with this one: 'I prefer to be a citizen of the World rather than of any country.'" Fortune, May 18, 1981.

The New Times, June, 1981, carried part of a paper presented by Jeremy Lee, May 23, 1981, at a Christian Alternative Seminar.

> "The anti-Christian structure on earth is a machine embracing many different parts, and spanning all spheres of political and economic spectrums, from communism to capitalism. It can be increasingly identified in the coalition of movements now struggling for the establishment of the New International Economic Order — a plan for the merging of all systems into a world government, in which one global system is consummated into a final ascendancy over each and all individuals. A glimpse of the shape of things to come has been provided by the **formal United Nations resolution banning Christmas.** The establishment of a World Government requires not only a meshing of all economic and political systems, but the establishment of a new world religion."

Don Bell Reports, October 23, 1981, indicated that the Cancun Summit was the first time that the two major thrusts toward a One World Government met openly. The one thrust is the New International Economic Order espoused by the socialist-communist regimes. The other thrust is the New World Order, the plan being followed by the capitalist nations.

"Premier Zhao of Red China stated on October 22, 1981 that the setting up of a New World Economic Order should start no later than early 1982." Daily News Digest, October 28, 1981.

2. I fear the President's Emergency Powers which a 607-page Senate report indicated: Senate Group Finds Near Authoritarian Status ... Must reading is: Emergency Banking Regulation "Restrictions on Cash Withdrawal, Chapter V." Also, about internment camps being set up in event of some emergency. The information I have received on this is too hot to handle. For more information write: Stanley Cronkhite, P.O. Box 5307, Polson, MT 59860. This same situation exists in Canada.

"Ottawa (CP) The federal government has assumed sweeping powers to control virtually every aspect of Canadian life in the event of 'vaguely-specified' emergencies. A cabinet order passed in May would even give Ottawa the power to set up INTERNMENT CAMPS for civilians in the case of war ... Ministers are being granted broad powers to act in a 'vaguely-specified' emergency. The regulations allow such moves as ... controlling food production, wage and price controls, and distributing food and other commodities." Edmonton Journal, July 18, 1981.

Everyone interested in the freedom of this nation should obtain copies of the Emergency Executive Orders. Your Congressman is one source.

3. I fear all United Nation Treaties! Especially the ones now awaiting Senate approval.

A. GENOCIDE CONVENTION. Senator Charles Percy is pushing this one. If passed, every Christian had better have a home away from home. The late Senator James Allen (D.AL) said: "Under the terms of the treaty a missionary could be tried before a UN INTERNATIONAL TRIBUNAL for the crime of 'genocide' on the grounds that to convert cannibals in Africa or New Guinea to Christianity is to 'destroy a culture.'" United States citizens could be hauled off by United Nations troops and tried by an international body for acts al-

leged to have been committed within the United States."
Spotlight, September 21, 1981.

B.   United Nations Covenant on Civil and Political
Rights. United Nations Covenant on Economic, Social
and Cultural Rights. Former President Carter signed
these two treaties at the United Nations, and they await
Senate approval; THESE CANCEL THE RIGHT OF
UNITED STATES citizens to own private property! We
have investigated these and have copies of them. THEY
do!

4.   ECONOMICALLY. I fear the Cashless System.

5.   SPIRITUALLY. I fear apathy on the part of Christians.

One Christian empowered by the Holy Spirit can change the
course of history. Dare to be used of God. Present your body a
living sacrifice.

Why Not Give Books Away?

QUESTION: Why don't you give your books away since you
are apparently wealthy?

ANSWER: (A member of the Stock Exchange in London wrote
twice, plus many others about this). We almost do;

FOR	WE RECEIVE
60%	.99
10%	1.49
10%	2.97
10%	GIVE AWAY
10%	$6.00 to $7.00 Contribution

For writing books, I receive nothing. I assign all rights to the Publishing Corporation, from which I receive no royalties, salary, or hidden expense accounts. The "love of Christ contrains me."

However, Paul did not give his tents away. Books are the works of my hands, like tents were with Paul. Enough must be realized to pay for a good-sized staff to market them.

Christians, I have learned something about giving. About 80% of my liquid income has gone to the Lord's work for many years. Sometimes, however, gifts are not valued or appreciated! People have registered or certified letters to me asking, begging, or demanding amounts from $50,000 in U.S. dollars to 30,000 pounds. Don't hold your breath! It isn't on the way. Six days shall you labor just like me! If you are unemployed, there is ground to plough somewhere which will provide for you. *"God opens His hand and satisfies the desire of every living thing." Psalms 145:16* . . . if we cooperate with Him. *"If any will not work, neither should he eat." II Thessalonians 3:10.* God provides for those who are willing to work.

An example which illustrates my point is: I received a call from a mother a few years ago. She was about to be put out in the street; her husband was chronically-critically ill; their everything was going to the debtors the following week. Foreclosing date was five days away. I did not know her, but she said the Lord spoke my name to her, and I was to help her. I offered to go on a note at the bank with her, and spend time assisting her in their business rather than give her the money outright. This I did, and their creditors were paid in full. They were able to keep their house, business, and land in the country as a result of this.

When the interest came due on the note, the banker couldn't get them to the bank — even to extend it. This went on for one and one-half years, and the banker called me. I went down and paid off in full, plus thousands in interest. The banker wrote this person expressing what a friend I had been to their family, and since I was required to pay off their note, they were now indebted to me. The bank mailed me a copy. That was over one year ago. This family who lives locally, has not so much as called to thank me, not to mention discuss payment of any debt. (Neither have I called them). I made the mistake. The Lord wanted me to know that there are many who call themselves Christians who neither appreciate a hand out, nor esteem the giver. I once read that God made every person a steward over all that he could be trusted with.

P.S. Many times people have phoned and said, "God called your name to me: (one said at 4:00 a.m.) and you are supposed to help me." Now I reply: "God works at both ends, and He hasn't called your name to me!"

We give books to prisoners, elderly, and the poor. Unless you qualify, don't ask for a hand out.

Most Amusing Things

QUESTION: What amusing things have happened since you published, *WHEN YOUR MONEY FAILS?*

ANSWER: A. I received a letter from Enoch and Elijah. They indicated that they were awaiting the call to go to Jerusalem where they would witness for 1260 days, then be killed; and after three and one-half days, they were going to ascend back to heaven. (I have heard of others who profess to be the Two Witnesses). These people are so deceived.

B. I received a letter from one who believes he is Mr. "666," the antichrist.

C. I received a letter from a Communist who says the "Bible is baloney."

Sensationalism Your Motive?

QUESTION: Didn't you write about all that sensationalism just to sell books?

ANSWER: If I harbored any designs on the book, *WHEN YOUR MONEY FAILS*, being a bestseller, these took flight when the Lord impressed me to write the last Chapter on the revelation of Daniel's 70th Week to me, with the "Catching Away" of the Church in Mid-Week ... the most unpopular of subjects." To have omitted it, the sales rate would have doubled or tripled. But, the Lord required it of me.

The Lord quickened to me just before publication that if this book pleased Him, it would not please everybody; and that, He could not please the world though He gave His only begotten Son; and that JESUS, His Son, pleased only eleven of twelve of His hand picked disciples; and, I could never upstage that ratio; furthermore, the measure of success I would experience, would be commensurate only with the depth of criticism I could endure.

Why Bad News?

QUESTION: Why do you always write about bad news?

ANSWER: I have often thought of how pleasant, comparatively speaking, the call of God is upon the Blackwoods, the Spears, and Bill and Gloria Gaither. But, can the Clay say to the Potter, "I would rather be there than here?" The Lord spoke these words to me in January 1980: "You are to teach Current Events as they relate to Bible Prophecy." The command was so distinct and explicit that I arose from my knees where I was praying and wrote it down. Being "obedient to this heavenly vision," finds me taking prophecies which are precursors of Christ's Second Coming and scrutinizing them in light of Current Events. The examination shows the imminence of Christ's return ... to the natural mind, this is "bad news."

It seems almost ironic that a compassionate loving Lord would have allowed such a crescendo of evil in these last days that would have necessitated his "treading the wine press of the fierceness and wrath of Almighty God." But, in that God is going to permit these things, He took great care to explain to His followers much about these tremendous disturbances, so that when these disturbing things begin to occur, the Christians would not be disturbed. *"I have told you these things before they come to pass, so that when they come to pass you might believe,"* the Lord said often. Paul added, *"I would not have you be ignorant brethren concerning these things."*

The gist of the "bad news" is that the Prophets and Jesus made it clear that before mankind would beat his swords into ploughshares he would unsheath history's most woeful weapon of war in the Valley of Miggedo; and, that while the thrust of this battle, Armageddon, will be fought in the land of Israel, its effects will be world wide. One verse of many which substantiates the scope of Armageddon is: *"And the slain of the Lord shall be at that day from one end of the earth even unto the other end of the earth."* *Jeremiah 25:33.* Verse 21 of this Chapter takes in all unnamed nations.

So it brings our arguments down to, "Why God?" About half of the Bible is written about God's judgments, which some say should occupy almost none of our attention, in that judgment is God's "strange work."

God is love, but He is just and holy. Those who refuse to accept His love, under His terms of justice and holiness, will be punished. There would otherwise be no reward for the righteous, and heaven's society would be no different from this earthly one.

The GOOD NEWS awaits "those who endure to the end." "What is this beating I hear in my ears?" It is from the Symphony of Peace. The Prelude is: From Swords to Ploughshares. The time frame is 1000 years.

"Until then my heart will go on singing,
Until then with joy I'll carry on ..."

Do We Have Apostles or Prophets in the Church Today?

QUESTION: Do we have Apostles or Prophets in the Church today?

232

ANSWER: God the Father contributed to the structure of the Church thusly:

> *"And God hath set some in the church, first apostles, secondarily prophets, thirdly teachers, after that miracles, then gifts of healings, helps, governments, diversities of tongues." I Corinthians 12:28.*

1. Apostles
2. Prophets
3. Teachers
4. Miracles
5. Gifts of healings
6. Helps
7. Governments
8. Diversities of tongues

God the Son (Christ) contributed to the structure of the Church thusly:

> *"And He gave some apostles; and some prophets; and some evangelists; and some pastors and teachers; for the perfecting of the saints, for the work of the ministry, for the edifying of the body of Christ: **TILL WE ALL** come in the unity of the faith . . . unto a perfect man, unto the measure of the stature of the fulness of Christ."*

1. Apostles
2. Prophets
3. Evangelists
4. Pastors
5. Teachers

. . . UNTIL WE ARE ALL PERFECT IN CHRIST.

God the Holy Spirit contributed to the structure of the Church thusly:

> *"Dividing to EVERY man severally as He will." I Corinthians 12:11. "For to one is given by the Spirit*

233

the word of wisdom; to another the word of knowledge by the same Spirit; to another faith by the same Spirit; to another the gifts of healings by the same Spirit; to another the workings of miracles; to another prophecy; to another discerning of spirits; to another diverse kinds of tongues; to another the interpretation of tongues:" I Corinthians 12:8-10.

Thus, to say that there are no Apostles today is contrary to the structure of the Church as set by God to continue until the Church is "caught away."

NOTE:

• The Holy Spirit's gifts are contributed for "Part-Time" manifestation; as many of these on whom they are bestowed may be full time employees of the secular world, housewives, or mothers, etc.

• The Lord's gifts to His Church; Apostles, Prophets, Evangelists, etc., are full time gifts in the form of men and women. A person may have a "gift of healing" and be a full time factory worker, but not so with Apostles and Prophets; these are FULL TIME WITH GOD; not necessarily, "full time" with an earthly organization.

The Office of Apostles and Prophets has few applicants. The prerequisites are stiff; hours are long ... in fact the office never closes. Credentials of a Prophet-Prophetess:

"And there was one Anna, a prophetess, the daughter of Phanuel, of the tribe of Aser; she was of a great age, and had lived with an husband, from her virginity; And she was a widow of about fourscore and four years, which DEPARTED NOT FROM THE TEMPLE, BUT SERVED GOD WITH FASTINGS AND PRAYERS NIGHT AND DAY." Luke 2:36-37.

PROPHET-PROPHETESS:

• She was separated from society (the world) unto God.

- She served God with fastings and prayers seven days and nights a week.

CREDENTIALS OF AN APOSTLE:

"And in those days, when the number of the disciples were multiplied, there arose a murmuring of the Grecians against the Hebrews, because their widows were neglected in the daily ministration. Then the twelve called the multitude of the disciples unto them, and said, IT IS NOT REASON (reasonable) THAT WE SHOULD LEAVE THE WORD OF GOD, AND SERVE TABLES. Wherefore, brethren, look ye out among you seven men of honest report, full of the Holy Ghost and wisdom, whom we may appoint over this business. But we will give ourselves CONTINUALLY TO PRAYER, AND TO THE MINISTRY OF THE WORD." Acts 6:1-4.

- It was absurd to think the Apostles would get involved in "daily administration."
- They gave themselves "CONTINUALLY to PRAYER and to the MINISTRY OF THE WORD."

It is a trick of the devil that modern day Preachers have given themselves continually to "daily administration." When the Word they preach does not go *"forth in power and in the Holy Ghost, and much assurance." (I Thessalonians 1:5)* blame it on "daily administration."

And, now to those who can receive this, as Jesus would often say, and hath ears to hear, let him hear. If you cannot find the meat in this, throw the bones away. I believe that it is very difficult to be an Apostle or a Prophet and have small children. To give oneself CONTINUALLY to God would be to the neglect of children, which would be displeasing to God.

I believe that it would be more difficult for a married woman to be a Prophetess, to give herself continually to God would be totally unacceptable to her husband, and displeasing to God. A wife cannot by-pass submitting herself to her husband's desires for food on the table, and fellowship, and still be pleasing to God.

I have been young; now I am older. I have been married; now

I am widowed. It would be an absolute impossibility for me to be a wife, and be married to the Lord in the dimension I have experienced since my husband's death. In the first place, I loved my husband too much to have separated myself 12-16 hours a day in study, and have my nights to pray and talk with the Lord. In the second place, had I done this, he would have "departed"; and unless I could have Brightened The Corner where I lived within Scriptural guidelines, it is unlikely that God would have used me in some less important place than my home.

For whatever office the Lord may have called me, lowly or great, I have been separated unto Him totally, without reservation, since my husband's death five years ago, I was only 47. I could have chosen to find my niche as a prominent member of society, even the jet set. I could have chosen to enjoy a safari, or to cruise in yachts. I could have taken up sail-boating; or I could have

> Flown the oceans in my own plane,
> And seen the jungles wet with rain ...

which I had done with my husband. But, the choice was not mine to make. Three weeks before my husband's death the Lord spoke to me:

> "I have redeemed you and called you by 'my' name, and you are mine.
> You are married to me."

So, I chose rather to suffer the afflictions of God's people than to enjoy the pleasures of sin for a season; esteeming the reproach of Christ greater riches than the treasures of this world ... I chose to "come out of the world and be separated unto God."

This kind of relationship I entered suppressed ALL appetites for money, fame, sex, and "Social Get To-Gathers." Believe me, I know this isn't for everyone! There emerged a relentless drive "to know Him." In pursuit of this objective I feel that I've gotten to know a few interesting things relative to total separation to God.

To illustrate this, the Apostles apparently had no children, and perhaps only Peter was married. Paul had less than an exalted view of both marriage and women. The Lord commanded Jeremiah to neither take a wife nor have children. Jeremiah 16:2. He also informed Ezekiel, who had a wife, that He was going to take her away, and he was not to mourn for her.

> *"The Lord spoke to me. Mortal man, he said, 'With one blow I am going to take away the person you love most. You are not to complain or cry or shed any tears. Don't let your sobbing be heard. Do not go bareheaded or barefoot as a sign of mourning. Don't cover your face or eat the food that mourners eat.' Early in the day I was talking with the people. That evening my wife died . . ." Ezekiel 24:15-18 GNB.*

Certainly some Old Testament Prophets were married, and had children: Samuel, for example. But the mixture did not work well. He was a great Prophet, but a poor Father. Of course, I am not advocating "imposed" celebacy. No organization could order this relationship, only God.

I challenge all of you single men and women. You have the basic qualification for being used of God in a mighty way. The prerequisites for being an Apostle/Prophet of God have always been, and will always be: CONTINUAL SEPARATION UNTO GOD. If you would give everything in the world to be like an Apostle or Prophet, you have defined the cost; everything.

CHAPTER XI

PREPARATION FOR THE LAST DAYS— SPIRITUAL

By far the most asked questions fall into two different groupings: **PART I: SPIRITUAL.** These have to do with questions like: How can I be prepared for the Lord's return? And, the second most asked single question: Tell me how to be saved?

Briefly, I could say; fall upon the Lord's mercy. Say, "Father, you are the only one with whom I have to do; against thee and thee only have I sinned; I confess my sins to you, for which I am so sorry that I repent; cleanse me with the precious blood of Jesus; put your Holy Spirit within me; and preserve my spirit, soul, and body unto the coming of Jesus Christ."

Of course this is over-simplified. Everyone who follows the Lord does much more. Is it not true that a person thinks little of being required to spend 16 to 20 years of life in preparation for a 30-year career on earth? Salvation prepares us for eternity; so we should think it not strange that more than just "believe and receive" is required. Conversion may take only a moment, but Salvation is a process . . . most people do not know the difference. The doctrine of Salvation is called Soteriology. It is probably the most needed, least emphasized, and over-simplified teaching in the Bible. Since I will be judged by God on how I treat it, I will take it step by step, the way I have learned it out of the Scriptures; the way I have experienced it; and the way I have taught it many times.

REPENTANCE:

1. **REPENTANCE** (There is no salvation apart from this prerequisite). Alluding to chief sinners and just sinners, Jesus TWICE said: *Luke 13:3, "I tell you, nay, but except you repent, you shall ALL likewise perish." Luke 13:5, "I tell you, nay, but except you repent, you shall ALL likewise perish."*

When John the Baptist came preaching,

"Repent ye," (Matthew 3:2) and bring forth fruits (works) worthy of repentance; (Luke 3:8). "The people asked him saying, What shall we do then?" (The same question people are asking today). He said: "He that hath two coats, let him impart to him that hath none; and he that hath meat, let him do likewise.

In other words, the welfare of the people would be taken care of when REPENTANCE from sin is practiced. It only became a government function because Christianity failed.

Then came also publicans, and said unto him,

"Master what shall we do? And He said unto them, "Exact no more than that which is appointed you."

Publicans were those who had paid Rome the highest bid to be able to collect taxes. They made their profit on the excess! John literally put them out of business when he said, true repentance will not allow you to exact (collect) any thing above that which is required by Rome. TRUE REPENTANCE would abolish many jobs today!

"And the soldiers likewise demanded of him saying, And what shall we do?" And He said unto them, "Do

*violence to no man, neither accuse any falsely; and be
content with your wages." Luke 3:10-14.*

John would not have survived very long in this society either.
Here he tells the soldiers who made their living defending with
swords, *"Do violence to no man."* This would have made them all
conscientious objectors! Some Army! Further, he added, *"Don't
lie because the government is your employer,"* (false accusation),
and, *"Be content with your wages."* To put it mildly, he wasn't a
union man. These things, folks, are the works of repentance. To
bring forth just the works of repentance would start a "Righteous
Revolution."

These are the missing ingredient in most people's conversion
. . . and the reason many fall by the way side. Unfortunately, these
will not likely be preached, because there is no way to make them
conform to a Popular Gospel. No one ever found a way to "dress
up" repentance and make it socially respectful and acceptable.

Come and lets visualize the King of Ninevah, as

> *"he arose from his throne, and laid his robe from him,
> and covered himself with sackcloth, and sat in ashes;
> and sent out the decree: 'Let neither MAN nor BEAST,
> HERD nor FLOCK, TASTE anything; let them not feed,
> nor drink water: But, let man and beast be covered
> with sack cloth and cry mightily unto God: Yea, let
> them TURN everyone from his evil way, and from the
> violence that is in their hands." Jonah 3:6-8.*

A despicable picture to the natural mind! This is the only in-
stance of aggregate repentance in the Scriptures. The scope of
this repentance reached to the ANIMALS who fasted also!

Now, let us remember, while this is not a pretty picture for the
natural mind, most churches are interested in numbers. Many seek
to fill their pews by scheduling celebrities, great musical presen-
tations, etc. But, this plain sermon Jonah preached holds a record
in NUMBERS converted. Furthermore, there was no expense in-
curred. The Evangelist paid his own fare, and required no advance
publicity. He was just a man sent by God speaking only a word
from God. That formula would still work today . . . and with re-

240

sults! If your relationship with Christ is less than a satisfactory one, try repentance.

RESTITUTION:

2. RESTITUTION

"And Zacchaeus stood, and said unto the Lord; Behold Lord, the half of my goods I give to the poor; and if I have taken any thing away from any man by false accusation, I restore him fourfold. And Jesus said unto him, This day is SALVATION come to this house . . ." Luke 19:8-9.

Sincere efforts should be made to pay debts to the uttermost farthing.

"Owe no man ANYTHING, but to love him." Romans 13:8

Restitution comes from genuine repentance which moves us toward expending our energies making up for times lost and wrongs committed ... "redeeming the time." With tenderness of God's forgiveness comes conversion of our energies from a previous destructive, to a constructive nature. Thus, we come into the state called JUSTIFICATION, which is the change in God's attitude toward the sinner.

Churches are filled today with dead beats, who run from, lie about, and refuse to pay their debts. The only people who have constantly "beat" me or stolen from me in business have been "professing Christians" whom I trusted, and to whom I gave more leverage.

I know of one "highly spiritual" man who stole from one of my businesses, borrowed from everyone possible, purchased as much on credit as he could; declared bankruptcy, and said, "Now that all the debts are out of the way, I am going into the ministry." When the world spews one out of its mouth, don't think the Lord will take him in unless he is willing to "make his paths straight." A couple of years later he called and left word that he had an urgent message about prophecy from the Lord for me. Of course,

241

I never returned the call. If he had a message from God, he would have had to straighten up his past, and I would have been the first to know it. There would have been an apology, and at least an effort to repay the money he had stolen.

CONVERSION:

3. **CONVERSION** Acts 3:19 *"Repent you therefore and be converted."* (Conversion is the human side of this spiritual change; when viewed from the divine side, we call it Regeneration). The Agency of Regeneration is the Holy Spirit. The great theologian Shedd explained: "A dead man cannot assist in his own resurrection." However, when he is quickened by the Holy Spirit, he is made alive, yet not his old self. He is a New Creature. *"Behold, all things are become new."*

   "It is a change instantaneous, secretly wrought, and known only in its results";[1] but, *"By their fruits you shall know them." Matthew 7:20. "Except you be converted . . ."*

4. **UNION WITH CHRIST:**

   ". . . Be you transformed by the RENEWING OF YOUR MIND that you may prove what is that good and acceptable, and perfect will of God." Romans 12:2. "Let this mind be in you which was also in Christ Jesus." Philippians 2:5. "Nevertheless, I live, yet Not I, but CHRIST liveth in me." Galatians 2:20. "If any man be IN Christ, he is a new creature: old things are passed away, behold all things are become new." II Corinthians 5:17. Lord Tenneyson cried for this experience:

[1]Strong, Augustus H., *Systematic Theology*, Valley Forge, PA, Judson Press, 1974.

> "O for a man to arise in me
> That the man that I am may cease to be."

Dr. Strong says:

> "Union with Christ has one legal fruit—justification; but, it also has one moral fruit—SANCTIFICATION." In synopsis he teaches that justification is instant and produces safety; "We are in Christ." Santification (separation) is the process and produces soundness; "Christ in us." Sanctification is distinguished from regeneration as growth from birth. *"That we may grow up in all things unto him . . ."* *Ephesians 4:15.*

Of Santification, Dr. C.H. Parkhurst said:

> "The yeast does not strike through the whole lumps of dough at a flash. We keep finding unsuspected lumps of meal that the yeast has not yet seized upon. We surrender to God in installments."

Horace Bushnell compared santification to the growth of a Christian thusly:

> "If the stars did not move they would rot in the sky. The man who rides the bicycle must either go on, or go off.

Faith Which Leads to Good Works

"Occupy (work) til I come." If conversion is known only in its results, then good works are inevitably the only means by which a Christian can be identified.

> *"What doth it profit brethren, if a man say he hath faith, but have not works? Can that faith save him? . . . For as the body apart from the spirit is dead, even so faith apart from works is dead." James 2:14 & 26.*

5. **GLORIFICATION:** Salvation is a process. It begins with repentance and continues through conversion, and santification until we see Christ. *"When He shall appear, we shall be like Him."* *I John 3:2.* Only then will the process be completed.

"For by GRACE are you saved through FAITH; and that not of yourselves: it is the gift of God": Ephesians 2:8.

Many today run to and fro and seek all kinds of mystical assurances of their salvation. Let it be known in all parts that there are no assurances of salvation apart from a knowledge of the "unmerited favor" of God and "FAITH" in the Lord Jesus Christ.

"The Lord is not . . . willing that any should perish, but that ALL should come to repentance." II Peter 3:9.

However, you can not work your way into salvation, although works result from your salvation. You can not weep your way into salvation, though you may find it accompanies repentance. Your mother or father can not pray you into salvation. Salvation is something you must initiate of your own volition. You must make the move toward God. You must "humble yourself under the mighty hand of God and He will exalt you in due time. Draw nigh unto God and He will draw nigh unto you." If I could repent and be saved for you, I would.

> "Could my tears forever flow,
> Could my zeal no languor know,
> These for sin could not atone.
> Christ must save, and He Alone!"

CHAPTER XII

"... Blessed is the man that feareth the Lord that delighteth greatly in his commandments.... WEALTH AND RICHES SHALL BE IN HIS HOUSE." Psalms 112:1-3.

PREPARATION FOR THESE LAST DAYS— FINANCIAL

The most asked single question in our mail bag is consistently: HOW CAN WE BE PREPARED FINANCIALLY FOR THESE END TIMES? Now it will be more so, especially in light of the death of the old Monetary Systems, with their respective currencies, and the rise of a New Money System, to be conducted with "Marks."

WHAT WILL BE FINANCIALLY SOUND DURING THE TRANSITION?

WHAT WILL BE SECURITY IN THE NEW SYSTEM?

What I am going to share has everything to do with Financial Health, although it will not involve the normal mechanics for prosperity, for we are in UNCHARTED WATERS. Prosperity (or security) for each Christian is unique, designed by God for that individual. Most Christians have missed God's best financially because His methods for them were not the accepted, approved, dyed-in-the wool means as defined by the world.

I have never dared teach THE GOSPEL OF PROSPERITY, but

I have for twenty-five years experienced PROSPERITY from following God's revealed plan for my own life. My financial health has resulted from recognition of and acting upon this.

Certainly, God is interested in us first spiritually, and subsequently financially. There is no way I could teach a Christian how to become financially healthy without emphasizing the fact that he must first become spiritually sound. So settle this now in your heart.

> *"Who shall ascend into the hill of the Lord? or who shall stand in his holy place? He that hath CLEAN HANDS, and a PURE HEART; who hath not lifted up his soul unto vanity, nor sworn deceitfully. HE SHALL RECEIVE THE BLESSINGS FROM THE LORD, and Righteousness from the God of his Salvation." Psalms 24:4-5.*

> *"The Lord REWARDED me according to my righteousness: according to the CLEANNESS of my hands hath he RECOMPENSED me." II Samuel 22:21; Psalms 18:20.*

QUESTION: Who shall receive the BLESSING? The one who has CLEAN HANDS and a PURE HEART.

QUESTION: From whom will this BLESSING come? From the Lord.

QUESTION: How big will this RECOMPENSE be? As big as your hands are clean.

QUESTION: How much will this REWARD be? Oh, it is commensurate with your righteousness.

Do not be afraid of the word righteousness, which means behavior that is just, without prejudice doing unto others as we would have them do unto us. IT IS TIME TO GET BACK TO ABSOLUTES. Some things are ABSOLUTELY RIGHT; some ABSOLUTELY WRONG; some ABSOLUTELY MORAL, some ABSOLUTELY IMMORAL; some ABSOLUTELY HOLY, some ABSOLUTELY PROFANE. Wisdom is to know the difference. Everything is not relative. King Hezekiah, on a death bed, could pray:

> *"O Lord . . . I have walked before thee in TRUTH, and
> with a PERFECT HEART, and done that which is
> GOOD in thy sight." II Kings 20:3.*

Need we add — God heard his prayer and extended fifteen more
years to his life. Earlier in his life it is recorded:

> *"And the Lord was WITH HIM (Hezekiah), and he
> PROSPERED WITHERSOEVER he went . . . FOR he
> clave to the Lord, and departed not from following Him,
> but kept His commandments." II Kings 18:6-7.*

Remember, we are dealing with the ONE who asked:

> *"Are not two sparrows sold for a farthing? (A farthing
> = 1/4 of 1¢). And one of them shall not fall on the
> ground without your Father's knowledge. But, the very
> hairs of your head are ALL numbered. FEAR YE NOT
> THEREFORE YOU ARE OF MORE VALUE THAN
> MANY SPARROWS!" Matthew 10:29-31.*

These last days do not negate any of the promises of God. They
are still "Yea and Amen."

We are interacting with this ONE . . .

> "Who makes the rose an object of His care,
> Who guides the eagle through the pathless air . . .
> Oh yes, your Heavenly Father watches over you!"

And in watching over you, He rewards you according to the
cleanness of your hands!

How sad, so many Christians have never learned HOW TO HEAR
FROM GOD. They do not know how to receive guidance from
God. Some do not believe that you can get specific with God. But,
these are absolute prerequisites for a Christian's health; (spiritual
and financial for any time), but especially in these last times. Because of this, I am going to share some of the ways I have both
asked of and received from God specific guidance, which is solely
responsible for twenty-five years of respectable financial health.
I will confine this however, to the year 1981.

Perhaps there will be those who will be totally "turned off" being so far removed from the reality of God, that they refuse to believe one can "ask and receive, seek and find, knock and have it opened." The things I share are true, contain no overstatements or exaggeration. They are written prayerfully, "for your admonition upon whom the ends of the world have come." Many of you will need to know God, "the One able to do exceedingly, abundantly, above all that we can ask or think," in this dimension in the days which are ahead.

Proving God in '81

I could start in 1958 when God "showed" me the business into which He was calling me. It was one about which I had never heard. I subsequently pioneered that industry in Alabama, and fourteen years later built the state's largest institution of its kind. These things were supernaturally "revealed" to me and they had everything to do with my over-all financial success. Perhaps these things will become the contents of another book. But, let me add that at the time God called me into business, I was an accountant, and had less than no expectation that I would ever be a business woman. I was seeking God every day about becoming a foreign missionary.

The financial times of 1958 and 1982 are quite different, the only constant being God; the One who *"giveth thee power to get wealth."* *Deuteronomy 8:18.* However, for the sake of brevity, I will share only up-to-date financial directions which I have received of the Lord.

The year was 1981. The economy seemed to be coming apart at the seams; the dollar fell to 5¢ of its 1940 value; bankruptcies in businesses reached an all time high, and interest rates hovered near 20% the majority of the year. Astute forecasters warned about Money Market Funds being risky, possible delays and even moratoriums on maturities of Treasury instruments; 70% of the Savings and Loans were losing money; big banks were at an all-time low in deposit-loan ratios, and the bond market lost 1.3 trillion which in itself made the stock market crash in 1929 seem like a picnic. Merrill Lynch blushed for weeks after recommending "bonds, bonds," only to see record losses continue to mount.

Cash surplus which I would have let draw interest in years past, I invested in houses and land ... always paying for purchases in full, and withholding sufficient liquidity to insure against borrowing money at high interest rates. I believe God's people should be *"lenders not borrowers, the head and not the tail." Deuteronomy 28:12-13.* I had already proven Deuteronomy 28 ...

> *"If thou shalt harken deligently unto the voice of the Lord thy God, to observe and to do all His commandments ... all these blessings shall come on thee and OVERTAKE thee." Deuteronomy 28:1-2.*

I was "gullible" enough in 1959 to say, "I believe, I believe God." All of my leadings from God since 1977 had been to reduce my involvement in management aspects, and spend 100% of my efforts in study each day ... about God, the Bible, history, economy, currencies, etc. I made such a clean cut with the past that I am reminded of Sir Isaac Newton. He discovered laws of light and gravitation, fathered differential calculus, and founded modern physics and mathematics:

> "... But all his serious scientific work was done by the time he was 42. He was then still strong and at the peak of his intellectual ability. For the rest of his life (he lived to be 84) he studied 'religion.'" Compton's Encyclopedia.

The encyclopedia hailed his genius, but termed his behavior "odd," since he pursued God the last half of his life with the same intensity he earlier pursued science. He finally discovered the source of all truth, God. Many have since, including myself. It makes all other studies seem like a pittance.

In June of 1980, after seeking God for direction in my studies of Current Events and Bible Prophecy, I arose from prayer and opened my Bible. My eyes became glued to a verse which looked as though it was raised:

"Write the things which thou hast seen, and the things which are, and the things which shall be hereafter."

For many years teaching/speaking had been my forte, but I had no ability to write. I recorded the notation, but had no knowledge of how to begin to put a book together. The same thing happened in July ... "Write." I resigned myself to the adage, "Whom God calls He qualifies"; so I received of Him whatever ability He chose to give me, and in six weeks I had the manuscript ready to mail for a book entitled, *WHEN YOUR MONEY FAILS.* I had no thought here that this book would transition me into another business, designed by God.

Copies of the manuscript were therefore sent to three publishers in late August 1980. Three days later I received a call from one. A contract followed, other calls, and a letter. But, the Holy Spirit restrained me from signing the contract. The greatest mistake I could have ever made was to allow this major publisher to do the book, but that was my heart's desire. This was the waterloo Satan planned and he used the weapon of "pride." I would have been proud to see the book come out under that label.

Disappointment is the more respectable term to use when I realized the Holy Spirit was constraining me to publish the book myself ... "Let Down" is a better term for my feelings. A major publisher doing the book would have not only satiated my ego; but printing, marketing, distributing—the publishing industry— was foreign to me ... another farm to buy, another field to plow, another vernacular to learn .. and at my age! But, this was going to be a business whose very product would sin souls to Christ; whose objective would be disseminating the Word of the Lord; teaching, reproving, rebuking, correcting, instructing in righteousness, building up, and edifying the body of Christ.

Praise God for "junk mail." An announcement came of a seminar to be held in Washington D.C. in early November, 1980. Its focus was "New and Better Ways to Print, Advertise, and Market Christian Publications." My associate and I attended. Understanding the "jargon" of the industry was my major obstacle. Fleming H. Revell's representative stood and spoke of the responsibilities upon her department in designing good jackets for new books ... "for jackets sell books," she said. I surmised that she was referring to book covers. Suddenly, the idea surfaced, that since I was publishing my own book, I would also have to design the cover. My impression of her expertise, and my lack of it caused me to notch "Let Down #2."

During the seminar, I migrated to people who impressed me in each field; space advertising, television promotion, and direct mail. When the proposition was presented to each that I had written a book, and was publishing it, "to a man" every expert declared: "An individual cannot publish a book and come out in the black." At this point I was just interested in a program which would move 10,000. That is the number I had ordered for a Limited Edition. One speaker, obviously brilliant in his field, made a statement in his presentation which I recorded for future reference:

> "Direct mail provides advertising and selling with built in response."

Three weeks later while assessing what I learned at this seminar, I read the credentials of this young man again who had spoken on Direct Mail Marketing.

> "In the Christian world, few people know as much about successful direct mail as Tom McCabe. And he'll let you in on the secrets. From finding the right lists, testing different packages, to rolling out with the big mailing. Direct mail can work for you and Tom will make sure you're aware of the basics that produce results."

I placed a call to Mr. McCabe. I was interested in his assessment on the possibility of using direct mail with my book. He was kind enough to give his advice free of charge, and honest enough to tell it like it was:

> "A book like you've written; about money, prophecy, would have to have substantial endorsements to sell ... If you could offer an as-

> sortment of subjects, with say six books, direct mail would pay off
> ... there is virtually NO WAY TO MARKET ONE BOOK, VIA DIRECT
> MAIL, and expect it to recoup expenses."

He was speaking of the norm. He was right on! Any book by an unknown author, who knows nothing of publishing, is a sure failure — except when God is in it. God's ways are not man's ways, neither are His thoughts our thoughts.

Starting with three typewritten pages, the design of the jackets began to take shape ... it became fun to reduce paragraphs to sentences and sentences to phrases. It took three weeks of condensing before I was impressed by the Holy Spirit, "It is finished."

With the book scheduled for release in Mid-January 1981, I accepted an invitation to teach on some prophetic issues while the Rev. Jim Thompson, of WGGS-TV, Greenville, SC, offered the book for a $25 contribution for his television ministry. He moved a few thousand which paid for the costs of the first Limited Edition.

My friend, Simon Peter Cameron, gave us the names of 9500 bookstores on pressure sensitive labels (over a year old), and we mailed out inexpensive flyers announcing the book. We made the flyers into envelopes, so that, as they travelled through the mails, they would witness to postal employees ... they did as calls and letters came in from mail carriers. (We were later told that virtually nothing sells through the mail unless it is stuffed inside an envelope).

The Rev. Louis Kaplan, of Jewish Voice Broadcast asked me to come to Phoenix in late January and do video-radio teachings. He offered the book on these programs. For the second time the response set a record, first with WGGS, then with Jewish Voice.

Having seen the response from TV, I began to contemplate the PTL and The 700 Club Programs. The Lord said "NO," so I refrained from contacting them. Simon Peter Cameron, my brother, Bernard Stewart, and I then met and planned for a two hour television "special," where I would do teaching, and Simon would offer the book. That night while asleep, the Lord let me see the entire two hour program at the station where we planned it. Then He said, "NO. I have a better way." I arose early and called both

Simon and Bernard and told them what the Lord had shown me. We cancelled it.

February 1, 1981, the Lord spoke to my inner man, "Cancel all speaking engagements. I will promote this book. I have a better way." February, March, April, and May — we cleared the slate. At the time when authors are beating doors down for publicity, I was back in my study, where God impressed me to publish a Newsletter, Current Events & Bible Prophecy.

The book became a bestseller in less than six weeks. In five and one-half months, we had over 600,000 in print. It was then I noticed the printer had never removed "Limited Edition" from the coupon in the back. Many mistakes in the book we just never had time to correct . . . for several weeks back orders ran in excess of 30,000 copies . . . not one dime had been spent in space advertising, TV or radio ads. Several Christian publications wrote or called about doing "reviews."

The Lord quickened me immediately that this was one of man's methods of selling books, and that I should send them a copy as requested, but write thusly:

"I respectfully request that you do not review the book in your excellent magazine, for any present assessment (judgement) on your part is premature, according to this scripture:

So then, men ought to regard us as servants of Christ and as those entrusted with the secret things of God. NOW IT IS REQUIRED THAT THOSE WHO HAVE BEEN GIVEN A TRUST MUST PROVE FAITHFUL. I care very little if I am judged by you or by any human court; indeed, I do not even judge myself. My conscience is clear, but that does not make me innocent. It is the Lord who judges me. THEREFORE, JUDGE NOTHING BEFORE THE APPOINTED TIME, wait till the Lord comes. He will bring to light what is hidden in darkness and will expose the motives of men's hearts. AT THAT TIME EACH WILL RECEIVE HIS PRAISE FROM GOD.".
I Corinthians 4:1-5. NIV.

Early the morning of July 10, 1981, a call came from Dottie Leonard of WindChimes in Nashville. She informed us that our book was the #2 bestselling paperback in the United States and Canada according to the Christian Booksellers Journal! We were such unknowns that CBA misspelled both the name of the publisher and the name of the author. By September, it had become #1; October, November, and December #1. I have been told that many major publishers have never had one book in the top ten. I had one book, my first, no advertising, and it became #1. Mr. Mel Berg, a Major Mid-Western Distributor said to me, "This book is a miracle of miracles."

God's better way entailed a network of housewives, business people, bankers, and brokers, who became distributors of the book, and purchased the book by the cases.

As 1981 closed, this infant operation had mailed out in excess of 3 million gospel messages via books, newsletters, tapes, etc. This printed ministry had circled the globe in eleven months. Souls were being won to the Lord literally around the world; translations were being made; all bills were paid; there had been no need to borrow, beg, or solicit contributions. Just a need to "Trust and Obey." Our staff, numbered up to 18 at times, worked 12 hours many days. The only thing we had going for us was one little paperback, a Newsletter, and God. A favorite chorus comes to mind:

> "Got any rivers you think are uncrossable,
> Got any mountains you can't tunnel through,
> God specializes in things thought impossible,
> He can do what no one else can do."

If God could do this in 1981, while the economy was crumbling, He can do this when it collapses, or when there is no economy, or when money fails, or most importantly, when The New Money System emerges. His Economic System makes earth's offerings look cheap. It is He *"that gives thee power to get wealth"* in good times and bad. The methods of acquisition differ, so it is imperative to always walk softly before the Lord, and be sensitive to His unorthodox designs, which make little sense to the natural mind. GOD USES SINGERS FOR SOLDIERS; AND TRUMPETS, PITCHERS AND LAMPS FOR SWORDS, AND WINS WARS! Read

II Chronicles 20, and Judges 6.

Paul was equally amazed that God's ways are "past finding out," and exclaimed:

> *"I stand amazed at the fathomless wealth of God's wisdom and God's knowledge. HOW COULD MAN EVER UNDERSTAND HIS REASONS FOR ACTION, OR EXPLAIN HIS METHODS OF WORKING? For: Who hath known the mind of the Lord? Or who hath been his counsellor? Or who hath first given to him, and it shall be recompensed unto him again? For everything began with him, continues its existence because of him, and ends in him. To him be the glory for ever, amen." Romans 11:33-36. Phillip's Modern English.*

Paul indicated time and again that the mysterious ways of God (which pertained to his life and ministry) God revealed to him. Likewise, Jesus Himself made it clear that the things which have to do with the lives and ministries of His followers will be revealed to them:

Address Q70059$$C2   Gal. (9)

> *"Because it is given unto you to know the mysteries of the kingdom of heaven." Matthew 13:11.*

I believe that God MAINTAINS something like a portfolio on every Christian. He only acts as a Chief Broker as one yields to His leadings. I know that God has MANAGED my portfolio for the past twenty-five years. There were years when my offerings exceeded my liquid income, but the value of assets so appreciated that my overall net worth increased. In spite of my high percentage of giving, the Lord has increased my worth on an average of 100% a year over the past twenty years. Yielding to God's leadings appear paradoxical. The natural mind will never figure it out.

> Lose to gain,
> Give to receive,
> Scatter to gather,
> Die to live.

Perhaps by sharing a couple of practical applications, one can see the fallacy of academic investments in the absence of divine guidance.

CHAPTER XIII

"Behold, the eye of the Lord is upon them that fear him, upon them that hope in his mercy: To deliver their soul from death, and to keep them alive in famine." Psalms 33:18-19.

INVESTMENTS FOR YOU IN '82

Some one more brilliant than I said:

"The mechanics of Economics determine War and Peace, Boom and Bust,

Prosperity and Poverty,

And woe to the Unprepared."

A friend called yesterday complaining about the Stock Market and asking if I thought she should get out. Let us consider that January 1981, the Dow Jones Industrial Average was 1003; it soon declined to 970. "If measured in 1940 dollars, it would be 46," states Dr. Franz Pick, World Currency Authority. In November 1981, it was down to 840. One famous or infamous advisor urged that his clients forsake the Stock Market in December 1980. While the press laughed him to scorn, the ones who acted upon his advice are probably healthier financially.

Let this be a rule of thumb for whether or not to invest in stocks. Check out the long term debt of the corporation. Investors holding stocks in 1929 which owed little came out smelling like a rose. DuPont owed only 15¢ per share; today they owe $8.30 per share; General Motors (discussed earlier) owed nothing in long term debt per share in 1929; in 1980 they owed $4.06 per share. Other big names as U.S. Steel and American Can owed nothing whereas in 1980 these owed $26.46 and $37.46 respectively. If the depression was tough on big companies in good shape then, and it was; it will be impossible for them when catastrophe hits and debts are high. Penn Central's stock had a AAA rating the day they defaulted; $13 billion was owed to creditors, who received $2.1 billion, or about $1 in $6. In general, the stock market is a no no, unless you are astute in assessing the posture of firms; or unless God gives you divine wisdom. Secondly, holding tax free bonds is treacherous, as "municipal default" will become respectable ... it's a polite term for bankruptcy. In the history of municipal bonds, about 40% of the general obligation bonds in default have been held void. Hundreds of cities have defaulted on bonds in the past, not just the more famous New York City.

Dr. Franz Pick says:

> "Government bonds are certificates of guaranteed confiscation. The thousand dollar U.S. bond, issued in 1940, is worth only $45.00 in purchasing power today."

With many experts declaring that all "dollar denominated" assets will be wiped out, and the currency exchange ratio will be brutal, the pickings for investments seem slim. I do not believe we should all leave civilization and eat coconuts; neither do I believe every Christian family should become an armed battalion. We are the SALT of the earth, the LIGHT of the world, epistles read of all men. A minister friend of mine said to me today:

> "WISDOM IS TO FIND OUT WHICH WAY GOD IS MOVING, AND MOVE WITH HIM."

If we ever needed the Lord for guidance in our every move, we need Him now. A few things God has impressed upon me in the way of investments:

1. Become debt-free ... a borrower is a servant to the lender. Get free from the bondage of debt.
2. If possible, have living quarters debt free.
3. A small parcel of land could be of tremendous value in survival. In Mainland China in the 1960's, the average family lived off the yield of ¼ an acre of land. This average Chinese family had ten members!!

4. Invest in apartments or houses, moderately priced, which you can pay for; and which could be income producing when hard times hit. For example, if you are debt free, and have $30,000 to invest; on the short term, Treasury Bills would yield the highest, and be the safest. A Certificate of Deposit, FDIC insured, would be the next step down in return and safety.

However, let's say the experts are right; and the "dollar is perhaps the shabbiest currency in the history of money." And, like hundreds of times before with other currencies, the dollar will be cancelled. If this occurs prior to the formation of the World Currency, it will result in an exchange. Dr. Franz Pick, who has lived through, and studied many currency reforms, says: "We will have a new currency. We will exchange at least 100 — maybe 1000 — old dollars for one new dollar."

If our $30,000 were in T-Bills, or CD's, we would have (after a period of time — three months in Germany in 1948) either $300 or $30 new dollars with this exchange ratio. I believe a place suitable for renting out which cost $30,000 before the crash would be more valuable than the new dollars. It would certainly be income producing, though it would be adjusted to the new currency values.

Any of the necessities of life; shelter, food, clothing, tools, cars, parts, etc. would be of more value than cancelled dollars. I feel strongly that every person should have some junk silver (pre-1965 silver dimes, quarters, and halves), and small denomination gold coins, preferably ¼ to 1/10 ounce Krugerrands ... Not so much for investment, but to have an established means of conducting business when money fails. Gold and silver dealers may be found in the Wall Street Journal, or in the Yellow Pages. Always get at least two different quotes before purchasing coins.

Basic to a Christian's investment philosophy is: Security is not in things, but a person. His name is Jesus Christ. He is primarily interested in the Gospel being preached in all the world. This has to be financed through the gifts of Christians who share this concern. I believe that the prosperity of every Christian is contingent upon his willingness to give anything at anytime the Lord impresses the need upon Him. When the burden of a lost soul — lost for eternity—reaches the heart of a Christian, new cars, clothes, homes, etc., are of little interest to him. FLAMBOYANCE AND CHRISTIANITY ARE AS TOTALLY INCOMPATIBLE AS RIGHTEOUSNESS AND UNRIGHTEOUSNESS! Repeat that sentence a few times.

When the time draws near for the full implementation of the New Money System, (the Marking-Cashless 666 System); or, when the Man of Sin is revealed; you will be able to discern this time:

> *"But of the times and seasons brethren, you have no need that I write unto you . . . You brethren are not in darkness that that day shall overtake you as a thief."*
> *I Thessalonians 5:1-4.*

It may be that a Christian can prepay necessary expenses, as land taxes, and maybe utilities, for a few years. Christians must at this time be debt-free and as self-sufficient as possible. Barter may be the only means of conducting commerce among Christians.

The "Mark" of the beast will definitely be required prior to the Christians' being "caught away," one way or another. Daniel 7:21 and Revelation 13:7. The war which the antichrist will wage against Christians during the Great Tribulation will therefore be economic; refusing them the privilege of "Buying and Selling."

I wanted so much to believe that the "Mark" would not be required until Mid-Week, about the time when the Christians will be "caught away." But, the Holy Spirit quickened me that just before the Wrath of God is poured out in Revelation 15:1, John saw:

> *"Them that had gotten the victory over the beast, and over his image, and over his MARK, and over the number of his name . . ."*

John saw these safe, praising God at last. Indeed, that is what will distinguish the Great Tribulation of the end of the Age, from the tribulation of the first three centuries—the "Mark." But, praise God, for the Pre-Wrath rapture! WE ARE NOT CALLED TO WRATH;

WE ARE CALLED TO THE RAPTURE! WE ARE NOT CALLED TO EXTERMINATION (not all of us) BUT TO EVACUATION ... for:

> *"We shall not ALL SLEEP (die), but we shall all be changed, in a moment, in the twinkling of an eye, at the LAST TRUMP; for the trumpet shall sound, and the dead shall be raised incorruptible, and WE SHALL BE CHANGED."*

Christians will not face any more frightening situations than those who have gone before us. Elijah was so afraid of Jezebel that he prayed to die ... really, the only guy that wasn't going to! The three Hebrew children didn't picnic in the furnace; the lions were not detoothed or declawed for their rendezvous with Daniel. But, God gave grace when grace was needed—never in advance. IF YOU ARE WALKING WITH GOD, SENSITIVE TO GOD, FUL-FILLING GOD'S WILL EVERY DAY IN YOUR LIFE, GOD WILL WATCH OVER YOU, SUSTAIN YOU SPIRITUALLY, PHYSICALLY, EMOTIONALLY, AND FINANCIALLY, AND PRESERVE YOU SPIRIT, SOUL AND BODY TO THE COMING OF JESUS CHRIST.

My sincere prayer is that you will come to "know Him, whom to know aright is life eternal"; that you will be able to receive personal guidance from Him; that you will be able to recognize it; and that you will have the fortitude to act upon it.

May Christ, the Messiah, Son of the Living God reveal Himself to you in your hour of need, as you remember He is:

> Abel's Sacrifice
> Noah's Rainbow
> Abraham's Ram
> Moses' Rod
> Samuel's Horn of Oil
> David's Slingshot
> Hezekiah's Sundial
> Paul's Handkerchief, and
> Peter's Shadow!

As you become sensitive to the Lord's leadings now, you will have the confidence to act upon these in the perilous times ahead.

Gary Paxton's prayer expresses our need so well:

"More of you, Lord, More of you,
We've had all, but what we need,
Just more of you.
Of things we've had our fill,
And yet we hunger still,
Empty and bare,
Lord hear our prayer,
For more of you!"

CHAPTER XIV

GOD'S TIME CLOCK

What time do you really think is on God's Time Clock?

ANSWER: About two years ago I posed the same question to a senior statesman, and a dear friend, Dr. C.M. Ward, while we were having lunch. His reply was, "late, late." He continued, "the most important one verse in all the Bible relevant to the lateness of the hour; the imminence of Christ's return, and the end of this Age is found in Hosea 6:2."

> *"Come, and let us return unto the Lord: for he hath torn, and he will heal us; he hath smitten, and he will blind us up. After TWO DAYS will he revive us: in the THIRD DAY he will raise us up, and we shall live in his sight." Hosea 6:1-2.*

This Jewish Prophet Hosea is saying to his people, the Jews, that the Lord will in time, tear and smite the Jews for a period of TWO DAYS, (2000 years, II Peter 3:8); but, that He will heal and bind them up when these TWO PROPHETIC DAYS (2000 years) are concluded. More importantly, the THIRD DAY, the third thousandth year, (the Millennium Reign of Messiah the Christ on earth), He will raise the Jews up and they shall live in His sight.

The Lord used the Roman General Titus to smite the Jews in 70 A.D. We are closing in on the 2000 years when God will bless Israel above all nations; when the Messiah, Jesus Christ, will reign over this world from Jerusalem, and the Jews will be the envy of all people.

> *"Yea, many people and strong nations shall come to seek the Lord of hosts in Jerusalem, and to pray before the Lord ... In those days it shall come to pass that ten men shall take hold —out of all languages of the nations —of the skirt of him that is a Jew, saying, We will go with you: for we have heard that God is with you." Zechariah 8:22-23.*

For our precious Jewish friends who need this to be confirmed in the New Testament, Jesus said:

> *"Behold I cast out devils and I do cures TODAY and TOMORROW, (2000 years), but the THIRD DAY (3rd thousandth year) I shall be perfected." Luke 13:32.*

(Also, to people in need of physical healing, you can see here that Jesus declared He would be engaged in deliverance and healing for this 2000 year interim).

Isaiah saw Christ from a child to a King, but he did not delineate the 2000 year interval separating these postures:

> *"For unto as a child is born, unto us a son is given: (the conjunction 'AND' is separated by this 2000 year period), AND the government shall be upon his shoulder, and his name shall be called Wonderful, Counsellor, The Mighty God, The Everlasting Father, The Prince of Peace. Of the INCREASE (surplus) of his government and peace, there shall be no end ..." Isaiah 9:6-7.*

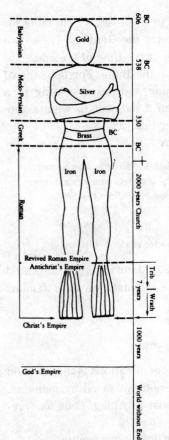

God did not confine His revelations of the end time only to Jews, however. A Gentile King, Nebuchadnezzar of Babylon, was shown in a dream the prominent Gentile Nations of the world until the supremacy of the nation of Israel was re-established. A young Jewish man was used to interpret the dream to Nebuchadnezzar. The head of Gold represented his Kingdom, Babylon, which in time would be left to the Persians, depicted as the breast of silver. The Persian Empire would be left to the Greeks, seen as a brass Kingdom. The Greek Empire would be left to the Romans, an iron Kingdom. In time the Roman Empire would become a ten-toe clay and iron Kingdom. But, when the Roman Empire was to be depicted by ten toes—there was no other place to go—the toes are the end. For:

"In the days of these Kings (represented by ten toes) shall the God of heaven set up a Kingdom which shall never be destroyed; AND THE KINGDOM SHALL NOT BE LEFT TO OTHER PEOPLE . . . and it shall stand forever." Daniel 2:44.

Most Bible students agree that the present European Economic Community is at least the nucleus of the ten toe Revived Roman Kingdom. Other nations may join; some may resign; borders of nations may be merged, but in the end the number will still be ten . . . IT IS TEN TODAY!

We are therefore not only closing in on Hosea's time table for the Jews, but on Daniel's time table for the Gentiles. These two time lines become synchronized here at the time of the end.

Now suppose one does not believe the Bible. For the sake of the intellectual, who is "ever learning and never coming to a knowledge of the truth," let us listen a moment to what astute observers of the secular world are saying:

The brilliant scientist, Isaac Asimov,

"... At stake is not one nation or another, but all of human history. ... The jockeying for nuclear 'superiority' is merely a race to arrange the precise details of the world's suicide." Next, June 1981.

Harvard's Harvey Cox adds:

"Mankind is in a plummeting plunge toward nuclear oblivion."

The Bulletin of the Atomic Scientists, January, 1982, indicated that there were four minutes before midnight on their famous clock.

The leftist Joan Baez recently said:

"We are all orphans in an age of no tomorrows."

The general concensus among leaders of nations is that the mid 1980's represent the most critical period yet faced by mankind. They speak of the world not as "post anything," but as "pre-apocalyptic."

A syndicated columnist assessed it like this recently:

"Whether you examine the diagnosis, or prognosis, the outlook is doom and gloom."

Paul said these last days would be characterized by PERILOUS TIMES. Jesus said,

"Men's hearts would be failing them for fear."

What time do I think it is?

It is just about time for our planet to rendevous with destiny. This world is in the sunset of its civilization.

Mankind is on a collision course with destruction. Our everyday headlines suggest that our world is hurdling out of control. We are in the TOES of this world's history. In the near distance we hear the drums of the last battle Armageddon. The day is far spent, night is at hand; Summer is ended, and harvest is past.

"O! Watchman, what of the night?
Watchman, what of the night?" Isaiah 21:11

At a luncheon in Paris in 1869, a group of renowned scientists began to predict what they believed would occur within the next century. A chemist, Pierre Berthelot, said, "By 1969 man will have split the atom and lit up the heavens." A physiologist, Claude Bernard added, "Man will be able to synthesize genes and create life in the lab in direct competition with God." One of the famous de Goncourt brothers, departed from scientific predictions with:

"I believe that before this time comes to science God will come down to the earth and say to mankind the way a bartender says at five O'clock in the salon, 'Closing time, gentlemen.' "

What a difficult concept for a simple mind to grasp, Closing Time for the Age. But, the irony is what sounds like the ringing of the DOOMSDAY BELL to the world, turns out to be the UNIVERSAL INVITATION to the saints of all the ages:

Come home, come home, it's suppertime,
The shadows lengthen fast;
Come home, come home, it's suppertime,
WE ARE GOING HOME AT LAST!

And now I pray that the Holy Spirit will quicken the words of truth to you; that He will bring you into a place of finely tuned fellowship with Christ which you have never before experienced; that He will impress upon you the lateness of the hour, and whatever you do must be done quickly; that He will fill you, control you, direct you, possess you, until you are no longer your own, but Christ's; and that from this moment on He will literally order your steps; place the same mind that was in Christ in you; make you victorious in all things; more that a conqueror; and that you henceforth will *run through troops, leap over walls,* and yet dwell in the secret place of the Most High God! Amen!

Sarah

Daddy

mommie

Drawn spontaneously by:
Sarah Elizabeth, age 4
My granddaughter
11-6-81

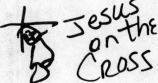

Jesus on the Cross

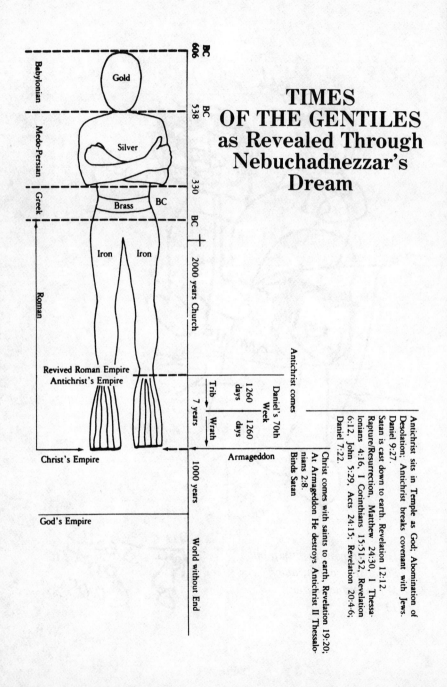

TIMES OF THE GENTILES as Revealed Through Nebuchadnezzar's Dream

BC 606 — Babylonian — Gold

BC 538 — Medo-Persian — Silver

330 BC — Greek — Brass

BC — 2000 years Church — Roman — Iron / Iron

Revived Roman Empire
Antichrist's Empire

Christ's Empire

God's Empire

Antichrist comes

Trib — 7 years — Wrath

Daniel's 70th Week
1260 days — 1260 days

Armageddon

1000 years

World without End

Antichrist sits in Temple as God; Abomination of Desolation; Antichrist breaks covenant with Jews. Daniel 9:27.

Satan is cast down to earth. Revelation 12:12. Rapture/Resurrection, Matthew 24:30, I Thessalonians 4:16, I Corinthians 15:51-52, Revelation 6:12, John 5:29, Acts 24:15; Revelation 20:4-6; Daniel 7:22.

Christ comes with saints to earth. Revelation 19:20; At Armageddon He destroys Antichrist II Thessalonians 2:8. Binds Satan

Partial Bibliography

Chapter II

[1]George H. Warfel, *Identification Technologies* (Springfield: Charles C. Thomas Publisher, 1979), p.137.

[2]Ibid., p.137

[3]*Wall Street Journal*, September 4, 1981.

[4]Nilson, H.S.: *Citibank's Secret Credit Card Encoding Process.* Nilson Report. Issue #95, July, 1974.

[5]Terry Galanoy, *Charge It! Inside The Credit Card Conspiracy* (New York: G.P. Putnam's Sons, 1980), p.205.

[6]Terry Galanoy, *Charge It! Inside The Credit Card Conspiracy* (New York: G. P. Putnam's Sons, 1980), p.176.

[7]George H. Warfel, *Identification Technologies* (Springfield: Charles C. Thomas Publisher, 1979), p.81.

[8]*Wall Street Journal*, May 21, 1981.

[9]*CCS*, Communication Control, Inc., 633 Third Avenue, New York, 1981.

[10]Dr. Ray Brubaker, *Is The Antichrist Now Here?* God's News Behind The News, Box 10475, St. Petersburg, FL.

[11]*Frost & Sullivan, Inc.* (New York, NY: 1981), p.141-ix-7, 9.1.2.1

[12]*Frost & Sullivan, Inc.* (New York, NY: 1981), p.140-ix-6, 9.1.1

[13]Penny & Baker, *The Law of Electronic Fund Transfer Systems* (Boston: Gorham & Lamont, 1980) p.9-14; p.905.

[14]*Business Week*, Electronic Shopping Builds A Base, October 26, 1981.

[15]Penny & Baker, *The Law Of Electronic Fund Transfer Systems* (Boston: Gorham & Lamont, 1980) p.1-12; p.1.01(4).

[16]Adam Osborne, *Running Wild* (Berkeley, CA: Osborne/McGraw-Hill, 1979), p.137.

[17]EFT In The United States, *The Final Report of the National Commission on Electronic Fund Transfers* (Washington DC, U.S. Government Printing Office, October 28, 1977) p.24 & 25.

[18]EFT In The United States, *The Final Report of the National Commission on Electronic Fund Transfers* (Washington DC, U.S. Government Printing Office, October 28, 1977) p.187.

[19]*Better Living*, October 1981.

[20]*Pittsburgh Press*, June 21, 1981.

[21]The Rev. David Webber, in *Point of No Return*, Southwest Radio Church.

[22]Interview of Dr. Patrick Fisher, as broadcast by Southwest Radio Church, Oklahoma City, and subsequently on Jewish Voice Broadcast Network. Most of interview contained in Southwest Radio Church's booklet, *The Eye Of The Antichrist*.

[23]Harvey A. Smith, *They're Rebuilding The Temple* (Hazelwood, MO: Dayspring Publishing Company, 1977), p.79 & 80.

[24]Electronic Funds Transfer Report, *MasterCard*, September 17, 1979.

[25]*Harry Schultz Letter*, September 8, 1980, Xebex, Box 134, Princeton, NJ: $25 a single copy.

[26]George H. Warfel, *Identification Technologies* (Springfield: Charles C. Thomas Publisher, 1979, p.11.

[27]Penny & Baker, *The Law Of Electronic Fund Transfer Systems* (Boston: Gorham & Lamont, 1980) p.15-18; p.15.02(2) (b).

Chapter III

[1]Salem Kirban, *Satan's Mark Exposed* (Huntingdon Valley, PA: 1981).

[2]*CCS*, Communication Control, Inc., 633 Third Avenue, New York, 1981. Bestseller, Volume 1, No. 102, October 30, 1981.

Chapter IV

[1]Richard Conniff, *Next Magazine*, August 1981.

[2]John Wicklein, *Electronic Nightmare* (New York: The Viking Press, 1981), p.248.

[3]John Wicklein, *Electronic Nightmare* (New York: The Viking Press, 1981), p.249.

Chapter V

[1]John Wicklein, *Electronic Nightmare* (New York: The Viking Press, 1981), p.27.

[2]*The Montgomery Advertiser*, November 8, 1981.

[3]*Business Week*, November 16, 1981.

[4]*CCS*, Communication Control, Inc., 633 Third Avenue, New York, 1981.

[5]*Wall Street Journal*, October 26, 1981.

[6]Pamela Weintraub, *Discover Magazine*, June 1981.

[7]Adam Osborne, *Running Wild* (Berkeley, CA: Osborne/McGraw-Hill, 1979), p.124

[8]*Hammond Almanac, Inc.* (Maplewood, NJ: 1981).

[9]*Business Week*, September 7, 1981.

[10]*Business Week*, September 7, 1981.

[11]*The Economist*, August 22, 1981.

[12]*Office Automation & Business Communications* Advertisement.

If this book, THE NEW MONEY SYSTEM, has been the means of bringing you into a saving knowledge of Jesus Christ, would you please write

Dr. Mary Relfe
Ministries, Inc.
P.O. Box 4038
Montgomery, Alabama 36104

Copyright 1981

WHEN YOUR MONEY FAILS 666

666 **666**

REVISED

UPDATED

FOR
CONTRI-
BUTION
OF
$5.00

The "666 System" is here.

The Government · The Number · The Card · The Mark

Kerman Scott Ltd.
666
60% POLYESTER 40% COTTON
PERMANENT PRESS
RED CHINA PRODUCT LABEL

666
EUROPEAN PRODUCT CODE

LEAR SIEGLER INC.
ISi **666**
U.S. PRODUCT SEAL

Mary Stewart Relfe, Ph.D.

* Bestseller in 6 weeks!

* #1 International Bestseller in 8 months!

* This book will grow more timely each year till Jesus comes!

* More current than when first published.

* EVERY CHRISTIAN HOME NEEDS ONE.

AT CHRISTIAN BOOKSTORES, OR USE ORDER FORMS IN BACK.

THE NEW

MONEY
SYSTEM 666

1982 Copyright

BEST SELLING AUTHOR

666

No Currency... CARDS

No Money... MARKS

Decode "666" in UPC

Sequel to

Read Actual Advertisement

Side A   Side B

*   WHEN YOUR MONEY FAILS is about the Number. THE NEW
    MONEY SYSTEM is about the Mark, and how the Number is
    incorporated into the Mark.

*   The Mark, in the form of a Bar Code, will become the means
    of required Identification in the Cashless Society, without
    which no one can buy or sell.

*   Those who designed the Cashless System will finally realize
    their ulterior motive. . .All the money of the world. This is the
    NEW MONEY SYSTEM. They will have the money, the public
    will have the "Marks." Then will be brought to pass the saying,

    "AND MONEY CAME TO PASS,
    IT DIDN'T COME TO STAY."

AT CHRISTIAN BOOKSTORES, OR USE THE ORDER FORMS IN
BACK. For contribution of $5.00.

CURRENT EVENTS

and

BIBLE PROPHECY NEWSLETTER

EDITOR: Mary Stewart Relfe, Ph.D.
ASSOCIATE EDITOR: Bernard Stewart, B.S., M.A.
MANAGING EDITOR: Sally O'Brien

GUEST WRITER

Dr. C.M. Ward
Prophecy Analyst

* IN DEPTH ANALYSES of key issues, especially as these affect Economies and Currencies of the world, scrutinized in the light of Bible Prophecies.

* EXCITING UPDATES on the worldwide "666 System."

* PLUS RECOMMENDATIONS in each Newsletter on how to prepare for Economic and Monetary chaos.

* OVER 1 MILLION MAILED IN '81   *   A BI-MONTHLY PUBLICATION

SOME OUTSTANDING ARTICLES IN 1981 ISSUES OF CURRENT EVENTS NEWSLETTER WERE:

HOW CLOSE ARE WE? • ARE THE SAUDIS REVERSING ECONOMIC POLICY?............................by Dr. Ward
BANK FAILURES LOOMING IN '81 • WHY INTEREST RATES WILL REMAIN HIGH IN '81 ....by Dr. Relfe
MONEY MARKET FUNDS — A TRAP • MORATORIUM ON INSURANCE POLICY LOANS ....by Dr. Relfe
FORMAL UN RESOLUTION BANNING CHRISTMAS • ASTRONOMERS FIND BIGGEST HOLE EVER.......by Dr. Relfe

PLUS many many more • This Newsletter is NEWS BEFORE THE NEWS • FOR CONTRIBUTION OF $15.00, tax deductible #63-0810862

Published by: MINISTRIES, INC. • P.O. Box 4038 • Montgomery, Alabama 36104 • 205/262-4891

★ OTHER BOOKS ★   PRICE EACH - NO QUANTITY DISCOUNT

CHRIST RETURNS by 1988, Deal
$5.00 paperback   _____ _____
NEW MONEY OR NONE, Cantelon
$3.00 paperback   _____ _____
YOUR MONEY MATTERS, McGregor
$6.00 paperback   _____ _____
SATAN'S MARK EXPOSED, Kirban
$5.00 paperback   _____ _____
ELECTRONIC NIGHTMARE, Wicklein
$15.00 hardback   _____ _____
TRIM FOR HIM, Cameron
$3.00 paperback   _____ _____

                                         _____ _____

NO	TOTAL ENCLOSED	_____ _____
★ DEBIT CARDS ★	SHIPPING AND HANDLING	_____ _____
ACCEPTED	TOTAL U.S. DOLLARS ENCLOSED	_____ _____

When using Credit Card, show number in space below

☐ Check Enclosed
☐ Master Charge
☐ VISA

When Using Master Charge
Also Give Interbank
No. (Just above your
name on card)

Card Ex-pires   Month   Year

SIGNATURE _____

POSTAGE & HANDLING:

TOTAL FOR BOOKS	Up to 5.00	5.01 - 10.00	10.01 - 20.00	20.01 - 35.00	Over 35.00
DELIVERY CHARGE	1.50	2.00	2.50	2.95	NO CHARGE

SHIP TO _____
        Mr./Mrs./Miss   (Please PRINT)

Address _____

City_____ State_____ ZIP_____

Ministries, Inc.
Post Office Box 4038
Montgomery, Alabama 36104 (205) 262-4891

BOOK AND NEWSLETTER ORDER FORM
UNITED KINGDOM ORDERS SHOULD USE THE LAST COUPON.

	Quantity	Amount Contrib.
THE NEW MONEY SYSTEM, Relfe Copyright 1982	_____	_____
WHEN YOUR MONEY FAILS, Relfe Copyright 1981	_____	_____

QUANTITY PRICES FOR ABOVE TWO BOOKS ONLY.

1 - $ 5.00	3 - $12.00	5 - $ 18.00
10 - $35.00	25 - $80.00	50 - $150.00

**CURRENT EVENTS & BIBLE PROPHECY
NEWSLETTER**, Relfe, 1 years subscription
$15.00   _____   _____

NO ★ DEBIT CARDS ★ ACCEPTED	TOTAL ENCLOSED	_____	_____
	SHIPPING AND HANDLING	_____	_____
	TOTAL U.S. DOLLARS ENCLOSED	_____	_____

☐ Check Enclosed
☐ Master Charge
☐ VISA

When using Credit Card, show number in space below

When Using Master Charge
Also Give Interbank
No. (Just above your
name on card)

Card Expires	Month	Year

SIGNATURE _____

POSTAGE & HANDLING:

TOTAL FOR BOOKS	Up to 5.00	5.01 - 10.00	10.01 - 20.00	20.01 - 35.00	Over 35.00
DELIVERY CHARGE	1.50	2.00	2.50	2.95	NO CHARGE

SHIP TO _____
Mr./Mrs./Miss   *(Please PRINT)*

Address _____

City_____ State_____ ZIP_____

MINISTRIES, INC. ● P.O. Box 4038 ● Montgomery, AL 36104 ● (205)262-4891

BOOK AND NEWSLETTER ORDER FORM
UNITED KINGDOM ORDERS SHOULD USE THE LAST COUPON.

	Quantity	Amount Contrib.
THE NEW MONEY SYSTEM, Relfe Copyright 1982	_____	_____
WHEN YOUR MONEY FAILS, Relfe Copyright 1981	_____	_____

QUANTITY PRICES FOR ABOVE TWO BOOKS ONLY.

1 - $ 5.00	3 - $12.00	5 - $ 18.00
10 - $35.00	25 - $80.00	50 - $150.00

CURRENT EVENTS & BIBLE PROPHECY NEWSLETTER, Relfe, 1 years subscription $15.00   _____ _____

NO
★ **DEBIT CARDS** ★
ACCEPTED

TOTAL ENCLOSED   _____ _____
SHIPPING AND HANDLING   _____ _____
TOTAL U.S. DOLLARS ENCLOSED   _____ _____

When using Credit Card, show number in space below

☐ Check Enclosed
☐ Master Charge
☐ VISA

When Using Master Charge Also Give Interbank No. (Just above your name on card)

Card Expires | Month | Year

SIGNATURE _____

POSTAGE & HANDLING:

TOTAL FOR BOOKS	Up to 5.00	5.01 - 10.00	10.01 - 20.00	20.01 - 35.00	Over 35.00
DELIVERY CHARGE	1.50	2.00	2.50	2.95	NO CHARGE

SHIP TO _____
Mr./Mrs./Miss   (Please PRINT)

Address _____

City_____ State_____ ZIP_____

MINISTRIES, INC. ● P.O. Box 4038 ● Montgomery, AL 36104 ● (205)262-4891

ALL CONTRIBUTIONS ARE TAX DEDUCTIBLE.
TAX #63-0810862

BOOK AND NEWSLETTER ORDER FORM
UNITED KINGDOM ORDERS SHOULD USE THE LAST COUPON.

	Quantity	Amount Contrib.
THE NEW MONEY SYSTEM, Relfe Copyright 1982	_____	_____
WHEN YOUR MONEY FAILS, Relfe Copyright 1981	_____	_____

QUANTITY PRICES FOR ABOVE TWO BOOKS ONLY.

1 - $ 5.00	3 - $12.00	5 - $ 18.00
10 - $35.00	25 - $80.00	50 - $150.00

CURRENT EVENTS & BIBLE PROPHECY
NEWSLETTER, Relfe, 1 years subscription
$15.00   _____ _____

NO ★ **DEBIT CARDS** ★ **ACCEPTED**	TOTAL ENCLOSED	_____ _____
	SHIPPING AND HANDLING	_____ _____
	TOTAL U.S. DOLLARS ENCLOSED	_____ _____

When using Credit Card, show number in space below

☐ Check Enclosed
☐ Master Charge
☐ VISA

When Using Master Charge
Also Give Interbank
No. (Just above your
name on card)

Card Ex-pires   Month   Year

SIGNATURE _____

POSTAGE & HANDLING:

TOTAL FOR BOOKS	Up to 5.00	5.01 - 10.00	10.01 - 20.00	20.01 - 35.00	Over 35.00
DELIVERY CHARGE	1.50	2.00	2.50	2.95	NO CHARGE

SHIP TO _____
      Mr./Mrs./Miss   (Please PRINT)

Address _____

City_____ State_____ ZIP_____

MINISTRIES, INC. ● P.O. Box 4038 ● Montgomery, AL 36104 ●(205)262-4891

UNITED KINGDOM ORDER FORMS

Books:

	QUANTITY	AMOUNT
THE NEW MONEY SYSTEM, Relfe £3.50 pence	____	____
WHEN YOUR MONEY FAILS, Relfe £3.50 pence	____	____
Continuous exciting updates in:		
CURRENT EVENTS & BIBLE PROPHECY NEWSLETTER		
1 years Subscription £9.00	____	____
TOTAL ENCLOSED	____	____

P and P 40 pence one book

Two or more books postage prepaid

Name _____

Address _____

City/Country _____

Phone _____

MAIL TO:
Rev. Simon Peter Cameron
New Hope Bible College
(Faith Acres)
Peterhead, Scotland AB47DO
Phone
011-44-779-83251

WHAT THEY ARE SAYING

U.S. NEWS & WORLD REPORT OFFICIAL — "Your book chronicles accurately the development of One World System of Government — Banking, Business and things related that need to be understood."

LONDON STOCK EXCHANGE OFFICIAL — "I feel most strongly that the details given should have a very wide circulation indeed." A.G. Levett, Associate Member, Robson Cottrell Ltd.

MID-AMERICA BAPTIST THEOLOGICAL SEMINARY — "Thank you for so much data and organizing it for the rest of us to study. . .What we see happening is a revival of ancient Babylonianism in this increasing use of "6" in computers, etc." Larry Walker, Ph.D., Professor of Old Testament and Hebrew.

EPISCOPAL CHURCH OF SCOTLAND — "I am finding many opportunities to pray with clergy and laity over the pressing issues of the end times. . .and really, your book is. . .by far the most helpful, especially in Biblical terms that I have read." The Reverend Alistair Petrie, Anglican Clergyman.

BUSINESSMAN — INDIA — "Here in India we are well aware of the moves to bring in the new world order. THE IDENTITY CARDS are on the way, having already been issued in some northern states. . .EVERYONE MUST HAVE ONE WITHIN TWO YEARS. . .I have already been assured by a banker here that the Clearing House for cheques for Indian banks in Bombay has the code "666." Don Stanton, Secunderabad, AP, India.

COMPUTER SCIENTIST — "God has prepared you to blow a trumpet loud and clear in this evil hour. Clear enough for those outside the Kingdom either by choice or ignorance; clear enough for those within the Kingdom who are asleep, and not busily redeeming the time while looking for His soon return." Patrick Fisher, Ph.D., Sidney, BC, Canada.